Contents

(continued overleaf)

Miscellaneous

The analysis of data from completed anaesthetic and surgical questionnaires is not included in full in this report. A supplement containing detailed tables is available free of charge from the NCEPOD office:

NCEPOD, 35-43 Lincoln's Inn Fields, London, WC2A 3PN

Telephone   0171 831 6430
Fax   0171 430 2958
E-mail   info@ncepod.org.uk

1996/1997

(1 April 1996 to 31 March 1997)

Compiled by

A J G Gray	MB BChir FRCA
R W Hoile	MS FRCS
G S Ingram	MBBS FRCA
K M Sherry	MBBS FRCA

Published 3 November 1998

by the National Confidential Enquiry into Perioperative Deaths

35-43 Lincoln's Inn Fields
London
WC2A 3PN

Tel: 0171 831 6430
Fax: 0171 430 2958
Email: info@ncepod.org.uk

Requests for further information should be addressed to the Chief Executive

ISBN   0 9522069 5 1

ASSOCIATION OF ANAESTHETISTS OF GREAT BRITAIN & IRELAND

✦

ASSOCIATION OF SURGEONS OF GREAT BRITAIN & IRELAND

✦

FACULTY OF DENTAL SURGERY OF THE ROYAL COLLEGE OF SURGEONS OF ENGLAND

✦

FACULTY OF PUBLIC HEALTH MEDICINE OF THE ROYAL COLLEGES OF PHYSICIANS OF THE UK

✦

ROYAL COLLEGE OF ANAESTHETISTS

✦

ROYAL COLLEGE OF OBSTETRICIANS AND GYNAECOLOGISTS

✦

ROYAL COLLEGE OF OPHTHALMOLOGISTS

✦

ROYAL COLLEGE OF PATHOLOGISTS

✦

ROYAL COLLEGE OF PHYSICIANS OF LONDON

✦

ROYAL COLLEGE OF RADIOLOGISTS

✦

ROYAL COLLEGE OF SURGEONS OF ENGLAND

Foreword

The information for this report, which covers the year from 1 April 1996 up to and including 31 March 1997, was analysed in detail by the clinical coordinators and advisors during the following year. The presentation of all the information differs from previous reports in that it concentrates on an overview and discussions of frequent or recurring clinical issues. It was approved by the Steering Group in July 1998.

The total number of deaths reported to NCEPOD for this study was 19496. Just over 47% of deaths occurred on the day of operation or within the next five days after the operation. Out of the 19496 deaths reported, 7097 (36%) of the patients who died were aged 80 or over. The number of cases for the detailed review was 2541 (13% of the total). These were subdivided into six groups of which four (head and neck surgery, minimally invasive surgery, oesophageal surgery and spinal surgery) involved consultants from different specialties, and two single subject disciplines (gynaecology and urology). The overall return rate of return of questionnaires on a purely voluntary basis by surgeons was 71% and by anaesthetists 76%. However, the rate of return by gynaecologists was 80% and by their associated anaesthetists 86%, by urologists 78% and their associated anaesthetists 80%. In each of the six groups of operations reviewed it will be seen that there was usually a high degree (over 90%) of consultant involvement in the decision-making and they were also often involved in the operations. Only 728 (43%) of these deaths were considered by surgeons at an audit meeting, and only 345 (27%) by the anaesthetists. These figures unfortunately do not take into account the fact that many of the reasons for, or the factors in, these deaths are similar and repetitious as will, I hope, immediately become clear on reading this report.

During the two-and-a-half year cycle of collection and review of the questionnaires and the publication of this report there have been many changes, or proposed changes, to medical practice. There is more emphasis on audit, openness and communication between patient, hospital and doctor, greater expectation of a successful outcome, longer survival with an ageing population. It is generally acknowledged that NCEPOD over the past decade has proved its worth and improved the standards of care by highlighting some of the deficiencies in the facilities, practice or provision of anaesthetic and surgical care. This is despite the fact that everyone involved in the preparation of the NCEPOD reports is acutely aware that the basic denominator data (numbers of patients and operations) are not available nationally.

Finally I would like to thank all those who have contributed to this report, from the local reporters to those members of the permanent staff at NCEPOD who work tirelessly behind the scenes to provide the data for analysis and are so ably led by our Chief Executive, Anne Campling.

V R Tindall CBE FRCS FRCOG
Chairman, National Confidential Enquiry into Perioperative Deaths

Acknowledgements

This is the eighth report of National CEPOD and we continue to be indebted to the local reporters and administrative and clinical staff who provide the initial data on perioperative deaths.

Many consultant and trainee anaesthetists and surgeons have, once again, voluntarily contributed to the Enquiry by completing detailed questionnaires.

The Steering Group members wish to record here their appreciation of the efforts of the NCEPOD staff: Peter Allison, Anne Campling, Fatima Chowdhury, Paul Coote, Jennifer Drummond, Sean Gallimore and Dolores Jarman. All data analysis was carried out by Sean Gallimore.

Recommendations

General comment:

It is a surgical skill to recognise when surgery will be too adventurous, ill advised or futile, given the condition of the patient. It is difficult to resist pressure to operate, whether this comes from the patient, relatives or medical colleagues but it must be recognised that surgery cannot solve every problem (page 38).

- A fibreoptic intubating laryngoscope should be readily available for use in all surgical hospitals. Several *anaesthetists* working in a department should be trained for, and competent at, awake fibreoptic intubations (page 27).

- The maintenance of an adequate blood pressure through the operative and postoperative period is an essential part of *anaesthesia* for patients undergoing carotid endarterectomy surgery. This requires invasive blood pressure monitoring and particular care in patients with poor cardiovascular reserve (page 33).

- Laparoscopic abdominal surgery may take place through a small incision but it still requires *anaesthesia* and the physiological onslaught of a pneumoperitoneum. High risk patients may not be able to tolerate this stress (page 40).

- Morbidity/mortality meetings should take place in all *anaesthetic* departments. Regular review of mortality following operations is an essential part of *anaesthetic* practice (page 123).

- There are many aspects around the care of patients undergoing *anaesthesia and surgery* for oesophageal disease, which are of major concern. A fundamental re-examination of the arrangements for the care of these patients is urgently required (pages 50, 57 and 65).

- The technique of tracheostomy should be taught to trainee *surgeons*. The indications for performing this procedure under local or general anaesthesia should also be taught (page 30).

- Pharyngeal pouch is a benign condition but appears to have a significant mortality. *Surgical* subspecialisation for this condition within otolaryngology departments is required (page 32).

- More detailed preoperative investigation and assessment may prevent radical spinal *surgery*, which is unhelpful for individual patients with advanced malignant disease (page 71).

- *Surgeons* need to be clear about the aims of treatment and benefits for the patient when planning surgery for advanced malignancy (pages 23, 73 and 76).

- Patients and their relatives need to recognise the limits of *surgery* in advanced malignant disease. A decision to operate may not be in the best interests of the patient (page 38).

- The hospital postmortem rate of 8% was unacceptably low. The reasons for this low rate need to be examined (page 95).

These recommendations have been selected from the report as it is felt that they should receive early implementation. Although the page numbers may relate to a personal commentary, in all cases these recommendations originated from strong views expressed by the groups of advisors. They are therefore based on the opinions of clinicians practising in particular surgical and anaesthetic specialties. As with all NCEPOD recommendations, in the absence of denominator data, they have not been statistically validated.

Data collection and review

The National Confidential Enquiry into Perioperative Deaths (NCEPOD) reviews clinical practice and aims to identify remediable factors in the practice of anaesthesia, all types of surgery and, from 1 April 1998, other invasive procedures. We consider the *quality* of the delivery of care and not specifically causation of death. Data are supplied on a voluntary basis; consultant clinicians in the relevant specialties are invited to participate. We also review requests for and reporting of postmortem examinations. The commentary in the reports is based on peer review of the data, questionnaires and notes submitted to us: it is not a research study based on differences against a control population, and does not attempt to produce any kind of comparison between clinicians or hospitals.

Scope

All National Health Service and Defence Medical Services hospitals in England, Wales and Northern Ireland, and public hospitals in Guernsey, Jersey and the Isle of Man are included in the Enquiry, as well as hospitals managed by BUPA Hospitals Limited, General Healthcare Group PLC (until April 1998), Nuffield Hospitals, St Martins Hospitals Limited, Benenden Hospital and The London Clinic.

Reporting of deaths

NCEPOD collects basic details on all deaths in hospital within 30 days of a surgical procedure, through a system of local reporting (see Appendix L). The local reporters in each hospital are predominantly consultant clinicians, but this role is increasingly being taken on by information and clinical audit departments who are often able to provide the data from hospital information systems. In the independent sector, hospital or nursing managers provide the data. When incomplete information is received, the NCEPOD administrative staff contact the appropriate medical records or information officer, secretarial or clinical audit staff.

Deaths of patients *in hospital* within 30 days of a surgical procedure (excluding maternal deaths) are included. If local reporters are aware of postoperative deaths at home, they report them to us. A surgical procedure is defined by NCEPOD as;

> *"any procedure carried out by a surgeon or gynaecologist, with or without an anaesthetist, involving local, regional or general anaesthesia or sedation".*

Reporters provide the following information:

Name of authority/trust
Sex/hospital number/NHS number of patient
Name of hospital in which the death occurred (and hospital where surgery took place, if different)
Dates of birth, final operation and death
Surgical procedure performed
Name of consultant surgeon
Name of anaesthetist

Since April 1998, NCEPOD has also begun to review data relating to interventional radiological procedures.

Sample for more detailed review

The data collection year runs from 1 April to 31 March. Each year, a sample of the reported deaths is reviewed in more detail. The sample selection varies for each data collection year, and is determined by the NCEPOD Steering Group (see Appendix C).

NCEPOD may collect data about patients who have survived more than 30 days after a procedure. These data are used for comparison with the data about deaths, or to review a specific aspect of clinical practice. Data from other sources may also be used.

The perioperative deaths which fell within the sample group for 1996/97 were those where the patient's final operation before death fell within the group of surgical procedures listed below:

Gynaecological surgery
Head and neck surgery
Minimally invasive surgery
Oesophageal surgery
Spinal surgery
Urological surgery

(For more detailed definitions of these groups see Appendix A).

For each sample case, questionnaires (see Appendices F and G) were sent to the consultant surgeon or gynaecologist and consultant anaesthetist. These questionnaires were identified only by a number, allocated in the NCEPOD office. Copies of operation notes, anaesthetic records and fluid balance charts and postmortem reports were also requested. Surgical questionnaires were sent directly to the consultant surgeon or gynaecologist under whose care the patient was at the time of the final operation before death. When the local reporter had been able to identify the relevant consultant anaesthetist, the anaesthetic questionnaire was sent directly to him or her. However, in many cases this was not possible, and the local tutor of the Royal College of Anaesthetists was asked to name a consultant to whom the questionnaire should be sent.

Consultants

We hold a database, regularly updated, of all consultant anaesthetists, gynaecologists and surgeons in England, Wales and Northern Ireland.

Analysis and review of data

The NCEPOD administrative staff manage the collection, recording and analysis of data. The data are aggregated to produce the tables and information in the reports; further unpublished aggregated data may be available from the NCEPOD offices on request. All data are aggregated to regional or national level only so that individual trusts and hospitals cannot be identified.

Advisory groups

The NCEPOD clinical coordinators (see Appendix C), together with the advisory groups for anaesthesia and surgery, review the completed questionnaires and the aggregated data. The members of the advisory groups are drawn from hospitals in England, Wales and Northern Ireland. The advisory group in pathology reviews postmortem data from the surgical questionnaires as well as copies of postmortem reports.

Production of the report

The advisory groups comment on the overall quality of care within their specialty and on any particular issues or individual cases which merit attention. These comments form the basis for the published report, which is prepared by the coordinators, with contributions from the advisors. The report is reviewed and agreed by the NCEPOD Steering Group prior to publication.

Confidentiality

NCEPOD is registered with the Data Protection Registrar and abides by the Data Protection Principles. All reporting forms, questionnaires and other paper records relating to the sample are shredded once an individual report is ready for publication. Similarly, all patient-related data are removed from the computer database.

Before review of questionnaires by the clinical coordinators or any of the advisors, all identification is removed from the questionnaires and accompanying papers. The source of the information is not revealed to any of the coordinators or advisors.

75	3	Ischaemic heart disease	Poor records		Returned to theatre with haematoma in the neck. Good recovery. Found dead after return to the ward, postmortem report not available to NCEPOD
82	3	MI, paroxysmal AF	Uneventful		CVA after return to theatre for bleeding from hernia repair done concurrently with carotid endarterectomy
74	2	Previous CVA	Uneventful		Ruptured intra-cranial aneurysm
63	2	TIAs. Occluded right common carotid artery and tight stenosis left internal carotid	Left carotid endarterectomy. Hypertensive during procedure.		Postoperative CVA

Grade of the anaesthetist

All the patients were anaesthetised by an experienced anaesthetist.

Consultant	17
Associate specialist	1
Specialist registrar year 4	1

Thirteen of the consultants were accompanied by another anaesthetist:

Specialist registrar year 4	1
Specialist registrar year 3	5
Specialist registrar year 2	5
Clinical assistant	1
Senior house officer year 1	2

Pre-operative assessment

Nine out of the 19 patients for whom anaesthetic questionnaires were received had the ward blood pressure recorded on the anaesthetic assessment form. The blood pressure was recorded before induction in 12 patients. In four patients the first blood pressure recording was made only after the induction of anaesthesia. It is difficult to manage a patient's blood pressure without knowledge of its usual level. All patients had the expected pre-operative investigations including ECG. Echocardiography was performed in three patients.

Monitoring

Monitoring of ECG, pulse oximetry and capnography was reported in all cases. Direct intra-arterial pressure monitoring was used in 16 cases out of 19, and in 11 of these, recording was started before induction. In one of the three cases where the blood pressure was measured non-invasively an arterial catheter was inserted but then became dislodged and the anaesthetist was unable to site a replacement.

Capnography was used in 18 cases, although in one case no readings were recorded. In five cases average end-tidal CO_2 recordings were below 4.5 kPa, in eight cases between 4.5 and 5.4 kPa, and in five cases were above 5.5 kPa. The patients had a mean age of 67 and a third had respiratory disease, so one could anticipate an unpredictable disparity between the end-tidal CO_2 and arterial $PaCO_2$. Nonetheless, no capnograph recordings were checked against blood gas analysis. The one patient managed without a capnograph had the blood gases measured on two occasions during their operation.

Cerebral function monitoring with transcranial Doppler (TCD) was used in two cases, and "EEG/Cerebral Function Monitoring" in another. Two patients were monitored with near infra-red spectroscopy (NIRS) and TCD.

Anaesthesia

One patient was managed with local anaesthesia alone. All other patients received general anaesthesia. In two patients this was supplemented with a cervical plexus block.

Many cases were marked by episodes of hypotension. Some patients were hypotensive throughout the operation. Four patients had marked falls in blood pressure after induction (one patient had a period of asystole). The management of intra-operative hypotension sometimes appeared illogical; small doses of vasopressors were given without effect and hypotension was then tolerated without any further intervention.

Grade of the surgeon (supervision in theatre)

Twenty-eight procedures were done by an experienced surgeon. Consultants were involved in the decision-making for all cases but were not physically present for two procedures* done by trainees.

Consultant	27
Accredited specialist registrar	1
Specialist registrar year 4*	1
Specialist registrar year 3*	1

Postoperative care

These patients require a high level of supervision continuing into the postoperative period, to monitor blood pressure and to detect impending carotid occlusion. Some patients were discharged from the recovery area to a general ward before their condition had stabilised. Is it not advisable that after operation all such patients should be managed in an area with at least the facilities of a High Dependency Unit, where intra-arterial monitoring can be continued for some hours after the end of surgery?

Record keeping

Record keeping was poor in some cases; it is difficult to understand such a casual approach to a potentially hazardous anaesthetic and surgical procedure. Is it wise to make only six recordings of the blood pressure in 2½ hours of anaesthesia? Automated record-keeping would be expected to help with the common clinical scenario of the anaesthetist trying to keep good records whilst carrying out several anaesthetic interventions. Unfortunately, the automated charts received at NCEPOD often had periods without any readings lasting several minutes, at times of cardiovascular instability. These gaps may have occurred when patients were being moved from anaesthetic room to theatre. Operative records were disappointingly poor and did not comply with guidelines for record keeping.[13]

Cause of death in all 30 cases reported to NCEPOD

Fifteen patients died from a stroke. Ten died from cardiac causes, four from respiratory causes, and one from rupture of an intra-cranial aneurysm. The postmortem examination of one patient who developed atrial fibrillation after operation followed by cardiac arrest showed that the patient had had a large myocardial infarction in the days preceding his operation. This patient also suffered from diabetes mellitus. Another patient had already suffered an established stroke and had aspiration pneumonia. His pneumonia worsened after surgery leading to septicaemia and death.

Conclusions

It would appear that in England, Wales and Northern Ireland, at the time of data collection, carotid endarterectomy was usually performed under general anaesthesia. Publications suggest that in North America a much greater number are performed under local anaesthesia. A review by the Cochrane Collaboration[14] found that whilst non-randomised trials suggested potential benefits from using local anaesthetic techniques, there are no good controlled trials to assist in deciding whether local or general anaesthesia is preferable.

Carotid endarterectomy poses important problems for the anaesthetist and the surgeon with patients almost always having significant concurrent medical conditions. Attention to the minimisation of risk factors for cardiovascular complications is as important as preserving cerebral oxygenation. The data reported to NCEPOD reflect published work that shows that approximately half the mortality from this operation is due to causes other than strokes. The care of many patients was exemplary. In others, it is impossible to say whether deaths would have been prevented by changes in the anaesthetic and surgical management but improvements were possible in

- pre-operative assessment
- monitoring
- peroperative management of blood pressure
- peroperative management of CO_2 levels
- record keeping

Minimally invasive surgery (excluding gynaecology and urology)

Key messages

- Minimal access surgery is not synonymous with a minimal procedure.
- Few deaths were related to diagnostic endoscopy but rather to subsequent major surgery.
- There was a high incidence of consultant involvement in decision making and operating.

Written by Mr Ron Hoile MS, FRCS in consultation with the minimally invasive surgery advisors (see page 11)

The term "minimally invasive surgery" covers a wide range of procedures (see glossary, page 109) and the sample included many procedures, such as gastroscopy and diagnostic thoracoscopy, which were simply a part of the patient's management rather than the final procedure (the specialties involved were mainly general and cardiothoracic surgery). In addition, many of these patients were elderly, frail with advanced malignancy or exsanguinating haemorrhage. A minimally invasive procedure was often used to obtain a diagnosis in the simplest way or in an attempt to arrest haemorrhage without major surgery. There were few deaths directly related to these procedures. However, these endoscopies often led to more major procedures from which the patient died. These subsequent operations and resections sometimes seemed inappropriate and aggressive. It is a surgical skill to recognise when surgery will be too adventurous, ill advised or futile, given the condition of the patient. It is difficult to resist pressure to operate, whether this comes from the patient, relatives or medical colleagues but it must be recognised that surgery cannot solve every problem.

Review of this sample produced several areas worthy of comment such as misconceptions about fitness for laparoscopy, the need to understand the indications for (and role of) a PEG, and the management of biliary stones in the elderly. These areas are addressed in short articles later in this section.

List of procedures

Procedure (may be multiple for individual patients)	Number
Percutaneous endoscopic gastrostomy (PEG)	17
Laparoscopic procedures	
Diagnostic laparoscopy (+/- biopsy)	35
Cholecystectomy	14
Inguinal hernia repair (two with adhesiolysis)	4
Gastrojejunostomy	2
Suture of perforated peptic ulcer	2
Adhesiolysis	2
Miscellaneous (one each of: loop colostomy, hiatus hernia repair, right hemicolectomy and drainage of retroperitoneal abscess)	4
Procedures following or as a consequence of laparoscopy	
"Open and shut" laparotomy	2
Open cholecystectomy	2
Miscellaneous (one each of: small bowel resection, pancreatoduodenectomy, re-exploration for bleeding, subtotal gastrectomy, division of adhesions, gastroscopy, Hartmann's procedure, oversewing of duodenal ulcer, Roux-en-Y repair of hepatic duct injury, right hemicolectomy and pyloroplasty)	11

Endoscopy

Oesophagogastroduodenoscopy (+/- biopsy or injection)	95
Endoscopic retrograde cholangiopancreatography (+/- sphincterotomy and stenting)	29
Rigid sigmoidoscopy (+/- biopsy)	27
Colonoscopy (+/- polypectomy)	20
Flexible sigmoidoscopy	13
Arthroscopy (knee)	5
Transanal endoscopic resection of tumour	3
Thoracoscopy	2
Bronchoscopy	2
Miscellaneous (one each of: arthroscopic menisectomy and percutaneous cholangiography and stent)	2

Procedures following or as a consequence of endoscopy

Laparotomy and oversewing of bleeding ulcer	6
Sigmoid colectomy (perforation)	2
Laparotomy for bleeding oesophageal varices	2
Transverse colostomy	2
"Open and shut" laparotomy	2
Miscellaneous (one each of: partial gastrectomy, right hemicolectomy, haemorrhoidectomy, laparotomy for gastrointestinal bleeding [cause unknown], sigmoid colectomy [volvulus], laparotomy for ileo-ileal fistula and drainage of abscess)	7

General comment

The majority of patients (80%, 250/310) had an ASA status of 3 or higher, i.e. were of high risk, and 62% (192/310) were over the age of 69 years. Deaths were mainly due to advancing malignancy and severe haemorrhage in the presence of extensive comorbidity and senescence. Most surgeons involved in these cases declared a special interest, which was appropriate for the case concerned; there were only 35/310 cases in which the surgeon perceived him/herself as a 'general surgeon'. The involvement of seniors was commendably high with 93% of cases having some input from consultants. There were 21 cases in which no consultant involvement was recorded. A consultant was personally operating in 66% (207/310) of cases and overall a consultant was the most senior person present in the operating theatre in 73% (226/310) of cases Direct comparison with other NCEPOD reports cannot be made but this appears to be a good level of consultant input. The advisors identified only one case where the grade of surgeon was possibly inappropriate; a case of iatrogenic colonic perforation following colonoscopy in which a laparotomy and colonic resection was done by a specialist registrar (year 3) after discussion with a consultant. Where the procedure was considered inappropriate it was the initial case selection which appeared to be suspect, coupled with a failure to adopt an holistic approach.

Another positive and encouraging area was the small number of cases where any form of non-clinical delay occurred (3%, 10/310); one could speculate that this may be due to the wider introduction of emergency theatres, often referred to as 'CEPOD' theatres. The use of audit and postmortem examinations in this group was also adequate with 74% (230/310) of cases undergoing investigation by a combination of local audit and/or postmortem examination as appropriate.

Specific consideration of the deaths following cardiothoracic surgery raised several general points. There were no deaths directly related to the minimally invasive procedures but the subsequent resections were sometimes inappropriate and aggressive. Two procedures in particular were considered to require direct consultant involvement. These were pneumonectomy in the elderly (over 75-year-old) patient with a high ASA class, and mediastinoscopy.

Minimally invasive abdominal surgery may not be minimally stressful to the patient

Key message
• Surgeons, as well as anaesthetists, need to be aware of the effects of peritoneal distension and the position of the patient. Despite careful anaesthetic management, unexpected physiological changes often occur.

Personal commentary written by Dr Ian Baguley FRCA and Dr Anthony Gray FRCA

Increasing numbers of surgeons and anaesthetists believe that laparoscopic general surgery may be advantageous in high risk patients and the elderly. It is thought that surgical trauma and postoperative pain are reduced, fewer respiratory and cardiac sequelae are seen, and the patients return to normal activities earlier. However, laparoscopic surgery can be associated with physiological changes which compromise both the respiratory and cardiovascular systems. These include high positive airways pressures, raised intra-abdominal pressure, and effects on venous return due to Trendelenburg and reversed Trendelenburg position, increased intrathoracic pressure, and compression of the inferior vena cava and iliac veins. Measuring, interpreting and correcting changes to these systems during surgery is essential but can be difficult.

Anaesthetic questionnaires were returned for 21 deaths in general surgical patients undergoing laparoscopic procedures in whom the pathology was benign.

Age	Operation	Days to death	Preoperative condition	Peroperative course
42	Laparoscopic cholecystectomy converted to open	1	Cardiac murmur, mild mitral regurgitation on echocardiogram	Uneventful anaesthetic. Cardiac arrest in ventricular fibrillation next day. Postmortem examination found no cardiac abnormality.
63	Laparoscopic cholecystectomy	3	COPD, untreated hypertension and ischaemic heart disease (graded ASA 1 by the anaesthetist)	Hypertensive in recovery ward. Three days later, severe hypotension followed after one hour by cardiac arrest. Postmortem showed pulmonary oedema cerebral infarction and severe coronary atheroma but no cardiac infarction.
63	Laparoscopic cholecystectomy	17	Insulin controlled diabetes. Previous CVA. AF, CCF, hypertension	Developed hypotension in recovery ward, admitted to ICU and treated with inotropes. Responded well and returned to the general ward, but continued to have episodes of cardiac failure and died.
66	Laparoscopic cholecystectomy	0	NIDDM. No cardiac symptoms. ECG showed some ischaemic changes	Became hypotensive on induction of anaesthesia, responded to ephedrine. Patient then stable until placed in head-up position. Became hypotensive with fall in expired carbon dioxide, progressing to cardiac arrest. Postmortem examination showed severe coronary atheroma.
68	Laparoscopy and drainage of abscess	9	NIDDM, poor general condition	Tachycardic throughout operation. CVA fourth postoperative day with progressive deterioration.
74	Laparoscopic cholecystectomy	1	Hypertrophic cardiomyopathy, AF, LVF	Previously turned down because of cardiac condition, but patient wished to proceed with surgery. Elective postoperative admission to ICU, but developed intractable LVF.

75	Laparoscopic cholecystectomy	9	Hypertension	Arrested on ward. Postmortem showed pulmonary emboli and severe coronary atheroma.
75	Laparoscopic cholecystectomy	30	COPD	Bronchospasm in recovery ward. Admitted to ICU 26 days after operation in acute respiratory failure. No information provided on events before ICU admission.
76	Laparoscopic cholecystectomy	18	Asthma. Angina, previous coronary angioplasty	Initially did well. Re-admitted seven days after operation with MI, and progressively deteriorated.
77	Laparoscopic cholecystectomy	10	Angina, hypertension, COPD	Hypotension intra-operatively when patient positioned head-up. Postoperatively required two unit blood transfusion. Found dead in bed four days after discharge. Postmortem confirmed presence of coronary artery disease.
77	Laparoscopic cholecystectomy	14	"? chest infection"	Intra-operative hypotension. Required doxapram infusion postoperatively. Developed LVF and bronchopneumonia.
78	Inguinal hernia repair and adhesiolysis	5	Angina	Left ventricular failure two days after operation. Developed intractable cardiogenic shock. Postmortem examination showed patient had had an MI one week before surgery which had extended.
80	Bilateral inguinal hernia repair	2	Fit	Hypertensive on return to ward. Hypotensive first postoperative day, treated with fluid. Cardiac arrest second day. No postmortem examination.
80	Bilateral inguinal hernia repair	11	Angina	MI second postoperative day. Developed LVF, and despite transfer to ICU on seventh day, died.
80	Laparoscopic cholecystectomy	8	Hypertension. Mild renal failure	Pulmonary embolus.
84	Laparoscopic cholecystectomy plus inguinal hernia repair	26	Previously fit	Initially did well, discharged on day seven. Admitted 12 days later with urinary retention, renal failure, DVT and pulmonary embolism from which he died.
84	Laparoscopic cholecystectomy	2	Mild CCF	Delayed recovery from anaesthesia, required admission to ICU, followed by an episode of sepsis requiring inotropic support. After discharge from ICU developed pneumonia and CCF.
84	Laparoscopic cholecystectomy	21	Fit	Labile blood pressure intra-operatively. Myocardial infarction first postoperative day. Subsequently developed left ventricular failure, biliary collection, renal failure, and gastro-intestinal bleeding. Postmortem showed moderate coronary atheroma.
85	Suture of perforated peptic ulcer	1	Angina, hypertension, with peritonitis	Two hour operation. Hypotensive five hours after surgery, transferred to ICU in LVF. Died 20 hours after operation. Postmortem showed severe coronary atheroma.
86	Laparoscopy and peritoneal washout	6	No information	No intra-operative problems. Died from peritonitis from perforated diverticulum.
88	Laparoscopic adhesiolysis	14	COPD, angina, renal failure, CCF	Operation for abdominal pain. Progressive deterioration postoperatively with development of pulmonary oedema.

The respiratory effects of pneumoperitoneum can be inferred from changes in ventilator pressure, expired carbon dioxide content and peripheral oxygen saturation. As muscle relaxation is generally used, changes to the pattern of ventilation can overcome the respiratory embarrassment. After surgery the reduced compliance of the chest and the increased airways resistance seen during pneumoperitoneum revert to pre-operative values within approximately one hour depending on the site and extent of surgery. Tests of respiratory function are abnormal only at the extremes of respiratory effort. Laparoscopic surgery appears to be suitable for patients with both normal and compromised respiratory systems, with only one patient in the table above dying from respiratory disease exclusively. Nevertheless, patients with severe respiratory disease may still be at risk of postoperative respiratory complications.

Respiratory events contributed to death in two patients; one died from bronchopneumonia, and a second from chronic obstructive pulmonary disease.

The cardiovascular effects of pneumoperitoneum cannot easily be detected by routine non-invasive monitoring. Changes in cardiac output and vascular resistance are not usually reflected in the capnograph, oximeter, ECG or blood pressure recordings.

General anaesthesia invariably produces a transient fall in cardiac output and blood pressure which most patients tolerate well. Positioning the patient head-up also reduces cardiac output. The introduction of pneumoperitoneum with direct compression of femoral veins and the vena cava further reduces flow, venous return and cardiac output. This may promote iliac vein thrombosis. The pneumoperitoneum splints the diaphragm which increases mean intrathoracic pressure, compresses the pulmonary vessels and increases the work of the right ventricle. Stimulation of the renin-angiotensin system contributes to an increase in systemic vascular resistance which increases the work of the left ventricle. The blood pressure is maintained or may even rise, giving the appearance that all is well even though cardiac output may be markedly reduced. Volatile anaesthetic agents which cause vasodilatation will ameliorate the increase in systemic vascular resistance. Vasopressors, when used to treat a decrease in blood pressure which has been caused by a fall in cardiac output, will further increase vascular resistance. These changes have been confirmed in both healthy and high risk patients undergoing laparoscopic cholecystectomy although the subject numbers are small and more research is needed.

These adverse physiological events may have been responsible for the episodes of hypotension and hypertension seen on reviewing the questionnaires. Laparoscopic surgery did not protect patients from developing severe cardiac complications during or after surgery. Many of these patients did not have overt cardiac disease when assessed pre-operatively.

In summary, laparoscopic surgery and its associated anaesthesia should be treated with respect. Recovery after laparoscopic surgery is probably improved compared to open procedures, but during the operation itself, laparoscopic procedures may induce as much physiological stress. Respiratory problems seem to be uncommon after laparoscopic procedures. However, when there is any suggestion of cardiac failure or widespread ischaemic heart disease there may be significant risk to the patient.

Percutaneous Endoscopic Gastrostomy (PEG)

<table>
<tr><td>

Key messages

- There should be careful patient selection prior to the insertion of a PEG.
- PEG tubes are inappropriate in patients with a very short life expectancy.
- A PEG does not protect a patient from aspiration of gastric contents.

</td></tr>
</table>

Written by Mr R David Rosin MS, FRCS and Mr Ron Hoile MS, FRCS in consultation with the minimally invasive surgery advisors (see page 11)

There were 17 questionnaires received concerning deaths after the endoscopic insertion of a percutaneous gastrostomy (PEG), 12 of which occurred within three days of the procedure. Details of the cases are given below followed by a commentary. NCEPOD has no information as to the number of PEGs that are appropriately used with advantages for the patient. The cases described below suggest that some clinicians are under the misconception that a PEG can be used to prevent aspiration of gastric contents, which it does not. In other cases a PEG was inserted in situations where symptom control might have been more relevant. Bronchopneumonia was often referred to as 'the old man's friend'. Is that statement still true in modern hospital practice or do we strive too hard to keep patients alive when the prognosis is hopeless and death is imminent?

Age	Indication	ASA	Comorbidity	Anaesthesia	Grade of surgeon	Day and cause of death
21	Brain stem astrocytoma.	?	Asthma & respiratory failure	LA + sedation	Consultant. Does 3/year	Died same day. Cardiac arrest
37	Carcinomatosis. Nasogastric tube not tolerated. PEG inserted for gastric drainage.	4		GA	Accredited specialist registrar. Does 20/year	Day 1. Carcinomatosis
43	Advanced carcinoma of prostate.	4		LA + sedation	Consultant. Does 6/year	Day 2. Carcinomatosis
50	Neurological problems (not specified).	4		LA + sedation	Specialist registrar year 4. No experience	Day 6. Pulmonary embolus and aspiration pneumonia.
61	CVA. No gag reflex	4		LA + sedation	Consultant. Does 6/year	Day 4. Cardiac failure and anaphylaxis (drugs)
61	Multiple sclerosis. Nasogastric feeding not tolerated.	4		LA + sedation	Consultant. Does 6/year	Day 7. Chest infection and septicaemia
63	Motor neurone disease. Unable to swallow. Nursed in GP unit.	4		LA + sedation	Basic surgical trainee. Does less than 6/year	Day 3. Aspiration pneumonia.

Age	Diagnosis	ASA	Comorbidities	Anaesthesia	Operator	Outcome
71	CVA. Unable to swallow. Two previous PEGs.	3		LA + sedation	Specialist registrar year 4 (supervised). Does 40/year.	Day 9. Aspiration pneumonia
75	CVA	3	Respiratory. Extension of CVA at end of procedure.	LA + sedation	Consultant. Does 12/year	Day 2. Progressive CVA.
76	CVA.	4	Carcinoma of colon, bleeding duodenal ulcer and peripheral vascular disease.	GA	Specialist registrar year 4	Day 16. Respiratory failure.
77	CVA	4		LA + sedation	Consultant. Does 5/year	Day 5. General deterioration and further CVA
79	RTA. Comatose with cerebral haematoma.	4	Demented	LA + sedation	Associate specialist. Does 50/year	Day 6. General deterioration
83	CVA. Aspiration pneumonia and dysarthria	4		LA + sedation	Consultant surgeon and anaesthetist present. Surgeon does 3/year	Day 2. Aspiration pneumonia.
85	Senile dementia. Facial fractures	4	Respiratory, cardiac, renal and neurological disease.	LA + sedation	Consultant. Does 50/year	Day 2. Aspiration pneumonia
86	Fractured femoral neck	4	Chest infection, ischaemic heart disease, cardiac failure and Parkinson's disease.	LA + sedation	Consultant. Does 30/year	Day 3. Bronchopneumonia
90	Multiple sclerosis	4	Chest infection	LA + sedation	Basic surgical trainee. Does 6/year	Day 5. Bronchopneumonia
92	CVA	4	Chest infection	LA + sedation	Consultant. Does 20/year	Day 7. Respiratory failure

Percutaneous endoscopic gastrostomy (PEG) has gained wide acceptance for patients who require prolonged tube feeding support. It is a well-established procedure for creating a feeding port in patients who are unable to take oral nutrition. The patients in this sample were often elderly, with multiple ailments and therefore mortality and morbidity was, in the main, due to comorbidities rather than the placement of the gastrostomy. Bronchial aspiration, which was a feature in many of the cases, is known to be reduced when feeding via a PEG but is certainly not abolished.

Benign disease

Procedure (may be multiple for individual patients)	Number
Oesophagogastroduodenoscopy	52
Oesophageal transection for bleeding varices	9
Oesophagogastroduodenoscopy and injection of oesophageal varices	8
Oesophagogastrectomy (rupture or bleeding)	6
Feeding jejunostomy	4
Repair of oesophagus (spontaneous rupture)	2
Repair of iatrogenic perforation of oesophagus	2
Miscellaneous (one each of: diagnostic laparotomy, partial gastrectomy, right hemicolectomy, sigmoid colectomy, laparotomy for postoperative bleeding, drainage of cervical abscess, vagotomy and pyloroplasty, drainage of empyema, revision of gastroenterostomy, laparotomy and repair of Mallory-Weiss tear, splenectomy)	11

These patients were under the care of a variety of surgeons, mostly general surgeons, who professed many differing interests. Of the 217 deaths under the care of general surgeons, there were only five cases where the surgeon specifically identified an interest in oesophageal surgery. Thoracic surgeons cared for 52 patients, a specialty where there is usually extensive experience of oesophageal surgery. In most cases the operating surgeon was a consultant (81%, 222/273) or a consultant was the most senior person in the operating theatre (87%, 239/273). In a few instances the grade of surgeon was not appropriate and comment on these cases appears below. Overall, consultants were involved in the care of 264/273 patients.

The management of patients with oesophageal disease (the majority of deaths occurred in patients with malignant disease) requires special knowledge, understanding and skills. This applies not only to the surgeon and anaesthetist but also to the large number of professions who support them and form part of the team (such as physicians, intensivists, nurses, physiotherapists, nutritional experts). A successful outcome for the patient depends on the provision of this team and the ability to offer a full range of treatments, supportive therapies and backup. Comment on the facilities for the specialist practice of oesophageal surgery appears below on page 65.

Questions arose when the details of the patients who died were reviewed. These included:

- What is required for the basic assessment of patients and their disease prior to major oesophageal surgery and how can this information be linked to a more holistic approach and an attempt at risk stratification?
- Can we improve case selection for surgery based on this assessment?
- How should anaesthesia for oesophageal surgery be conducted?
- How can the number of inappropriate, poorly conceived and often unorthodox operations be reduced?
- What is the current role of oesophageal transection for bleeding oesophageal varices?
- How should a department offering a surgical service for the treatment of oesophageal disease be staffed and organised?
- Is there any place for the open insertion of oesophageal tubes or stents?

These questions were prompted during the review of specific cases. Examples of the defective delivery of care are given below followed by broader discussion of some specific issues addressing the questions above.

Inappropriate operations

There were examples of inappropriate operations, often linked to poor decision-making in general. Some cases involved incorrect choice of procedure due to lack of experience or the inability to provide a wide range of procedures. In other instances there were illogical and unorthodox approaches to a problem or failure to acknowledge the frailty of the patient. Other cases demonstrated an incorrect choice of general anaesthesia for endoscopic procedures and, overall, there was a general absence of an holistic approach.

Age	Operation	Problems	Comments by the advisors
36	Oesophagectomy (achalasia)	Complicated case following multiple procedures. Died from haemorrhage on day of operation	Surgical plan questionable. General surgeon operating when superspecialist needed. Knowledge of thoracic anatomy lacking.
52	Oesophagogastrectomy.	Severe cachexia ASA 3.	Technical error using feeding gastrostomy for inadequate time preop. No staging or assessment. Not a suitable case for surgery.
58	Oesophagogastroduodenoscopy ?gastric volvulus. Later right hemicolectomy.	Died from multiorgan failure 19 days after laparotomy.	Inappropriate procedure, delayed diagnosis.
64	Initially three-stage oesophagectomy and splenectomy. Final procedure was feeding jejunostomy.	Recurrent tumour in upper third after irradiation. COPD. 17 days in ICU. Anastomotic leak. Died two days after jejunostomy – carcinomatosis.	Initial resection through tumour (operation seems illogical in view of previous assessment), technique described unorthodox. Decision to feed too late.
66	Oesophageal transection for bleeding varices.	COPD, IHD, hepatic and renal failure.	Patient was unlikely to survive.
67	Thoracoabdominal oesophagogastrectomy.	Incomplete resection. MRSA sepsis.	Gross disease remained. Better to abandon procedure.
70	Laparotomy to reposition oesophageal tube.		Endoscopic expertise to change tube not available.
71	Oesophagogastrectomy and division of pharyngeal web	Inadequate preoperative assessment. Incomplete resection.	Gross disease remained. Better to abandon procedure.
72	Resection of necrotic jejunal graft.	Oesophagogastrectomy. Free jejunal graft for reconstruction became necrotic. Resection margins positive.	First operation inappropriate and inadequate. 48-hour delay after leak recognised. ASA 5 i.e. moribund.
76	Attempt to intubate recurrent tumour at anastomosis two years after transhiatal oesophagectomy.	Cachectic (wt 30kg) and breathless. Cardiac arrest on table.	Poor case selection and unorthodox technique.
85	Laparotomy for open insertion of Mousseau-Barbin tube. Abandoned.	Elderly patient with extensive tumour. Died day five –carcinomatosis.	Outmoded inappropriate management. Palliation should be possible without open surgery.
86	Palliative bypass lower oesophagus via thoracotomy.	Previous total cystectomy. Died first postoperative day.	No attempt at endoscopic intubation. Careful thought needed in patients aged over 80.
88	Repair of iatrogenic oesophageal perforation.	Tear caused by endoscopic attempts to remove large gallstone impacted in pylorus. Death two weeks later.	Ill-advised endoscopic procedure.

Poor decision-making regarding intubation

Age	Procedure	Problems	Comments by the advisors
68	Oesophagogastroduodenoscopy and insertion of stent	Known liver metastases. Died six days after procedure.	Was symptom control more appropriate?
71	Laparotomy and insertion of Mousseau-Barbin tube.	Iatrogenic perforation of distal squamous carcinoma. Died of asphyxiation six days later when tube dislodged.	Fourth year specialist registrar operating without supervision. Postmortem examination showed operable lesion. Inappropriate decision to intubate a fit patient without proper assessment of stage of disease. No senior help available.
76	Oesophagogastroduodenoscopy and insertion of nasogastric feeding tube.	Repeated endoscopic laser treatment of tumour. Tracheo-oesophageal fistula.	Insertion of feeding tube delayed for 26 days. A stent might have been more appropriate.
80	Repositioning of oesophageal tube under general anaesthesia.	Very frail, ASA 4. Died 11 days later – carcinomatosis.	Why give a general anaesthetic? Was procedure appropriate for terminally ill patient?
80	Open insertion of oesophageal tube for stricture.	Large preoperative haematemesis, anaemia, thrombocytopenia and hypoalbuminaemia.	No mention that stricture was impassable. Was endoscopic treatment considered?
91	Oesophageal dilatation and insertion of tube.	Diagnosis made eight months previously. Difficult procedure. Died 15 days later.	Why give a general anaesthetic? Survival was expected to be short. Was this procedure necessary?

Case selection

Some circumspection might help surgeons identify those patients who were clearly not going to benefit from the procedure at the time it took place.

Age	Procedure	Problems	Comments by the advisors
37	Oesophagogastroduodenoscopy.	Perforated oesophagus. Died 14 days postoperatively	Young patient with vomiting and weight loss. Benign disease likely but inadequate work-up.
64	Laparotomy for lymphatic leak following oesophagogastrectomy.	Known cirrhotic. Died four days after surgery. Multiorgan failure.	Ascites not leak. Underestimated comorbidity.
66	Oesophagogastrectomy.	Bronchopneumonia and hypokalaemia preoperatively. Died 13 days postoperatively.	Cause of death was bronchopneumonia. This patient was not a suitable candidate for this operation.
71	Bronchoscopy and mini-tracheostomy following oesophagogastrectomy.	No tissue diagnosis before original operation. Extensive comorbidity with cardiorespiratory disease. Left lung collapse.	Death due to respiratory failure. Extent of comorbidity appeared to be contraindication to surgery.

Age	Procedure	Problems	Comments by the advisors
79	Ivor-Lewis oesophagogastrectomy.	Tumour inadequately staged and found to invade left bronchus and trachea. Resection palliative.	Poor preoperative assessment and subsequent judgement. Thoracotomy should have been "open and close".
83	Ivor-Lewis oesophagogastrectomy and splenectomy.	Thrombocytopenia, hypertension, ischaemic heart disease and aortic aneurysm. Anaesthetic assessment one hour before surgery.	Died from haemorrhage 24 hours after surgery. No cause identified clinically and no postmortem examination.
85	Oesophageal dilatation & insertion of percutaneous endoscopic gastrostomy.	Third attempt at endoscopy and dilatation in demented frail patient. Radiotherapy apparently considered.	Died with bronchopneumonia three days after surgery.

Inadequate preoperative assessment and preparation

Age	Procedure	Problems	Comments by the advisors
69	Oesophagogastrectomy.	Poor preoperative assessment in patient with ischaemic heart disease, thoracic aneurysm, hypertension, TIAs and peripheral vascular disease.	Disease understaged and resection margins involved with tumour. Subsequent anastomotic breakdown. Inadequate operation by occasional oesophageal surgeon.
70	Oesophagogastrectomy.	No antibiotic prophylaxis. Fast atrial fibrillation postoperatively due to anastomotic breakdown.	No preoperative assessment apparent from questionnaire. Inadequate management of surgical complication. No postmortem examinations. Implications ignored for six days.
78	Oesophagogastroduodenoscopy and injection bleeding duodenal ulcer.	Patient with dense hemiplegia, Hb 6.5 g/dl and no transfusion.	Lack of initial resuscitation and inappropriate endoscopy by inexperienced vascular surgeon. Died after rebleed at three days.

Lack of ICU beds or early discharge from ICU

Age	Procedure	Problems	Comments by the advisors
59	Transhiatal oesophagectomy.	High risk case with COPD, rheumatoid arthritis and peripheral vascular disease.	Surgery commenced without ICU bed available. Should procedure have been started? Died with respiratory failure.
67	Oesophagogastrectomy.	Preoperative chemotherapy.	ICU full so nursed on general ward. Chylothorax and anastomotic breakdown. Failed to reoperate when complications recognised.

Age	Procedure	Problems	Comments by the advisors
72	Oesophagogastrectomy.	Initially fine but discharged from ICU early because of pressure on beds. Chest infection with pseudomonas and ARDS. Readmitted to ICU on day seven after bronchoscopy.	Died on day 13 from respiratory failure.
74	Oesophagogastrectomy.	Fit patient not admitted to ICU until late stages of respiratory failure.	No preparation, no ICU, inappropriate anaesthetist, and surgeon had never done this procedure before. Died on day nine from cardiorespiratory failure.
75	Oesophagogastrectomy.	Known ischaemic heart disease. ECG changes noted during surgery.	No ICU bed therefore nursed in theatre postoperatively. Invasive monitoring inserted postoperatively. Died in theatre – myocardial infarction.

Problems with the management of oesophageal varices

Age	Procedure	Problems	Comments by the advisors
40	Laparotomy and insertion of Minnesota tube	Massive bleeding from varices with known metastases in liver (previous breast carcinoma).	Heroic and inappropriate surgery in terminally ill patient.
55	Oesophagogastroduodenoscopy	Massive bleeding from varices.	Research registrar operating. No attempt at therapeutic procedures.
57	Oesophageal transection.	Coagulopathy and hepatic failure. No attempt at endoscopic therapy.	General surgeon with an interest in breast surgery had only performed this procedure once before.
66	Laparotomy, stapling of oesophagus and gastrostomy.	Attempt to underrun bleeding vessels failed. Oesophagus divided and stapled off above bleeding varices. Died on day two from continued bleeding.	Wrong operation. No postmortem examination. Why not refer to specialist centre?
66	Oesophageal transection for bleeding varices.	COPD, ischaemic heart disease, renal and hepatic failure. Died on day four with multi-organ failure.	This patient was unlikely to survive.
69	Oesophageal transection.	Bleeding varices in patient with lobar pneumonia, cardiac and renal failure.	Basic trainee anaesthetist. Died on operating table. Inappropriate operation.
72	Oesophageal transection & splenectomy.	Bleeding varices and coagulopathy. No blood products given to correct deficiencies. No attempt at endoscopic treatment prior to surgery.	Inadequate treatment. Surgeon had never done procedure before and anaesthetist was very junior basic trainee.

General problems

Age	Procedure	Problems	Comments by the advisors
55	Oesophagogastrectomy.	Ankylosing spondylitis.	Poor fluid management with overload.
72	Total gastrectomy.	Preoperative chemotherapy. Anastomotic and duodenal stump leak.	Inexperienced registrar operating; not assisted by consultant.
74	Oesophagogastrectomy.	Adenocarcinoma in Barrett's oesophagus. Preoperative chemotherapy.	Surgical mishap. Splenectomy. Blood loss six litres. Poor surgery and poor management of blood replacement. Sepsis and multi-organ failure.
75	Oesophagogastrectomy.	COPD & CCF. Poor respiratory function measured preoperatively. Never came off ventilator postoperatively.	Inappropriate grade of surgeon and counselling/consent questionable.

Reoperation for early complications

Sometimes complications occurred, were recognised but then corrective surgery was either delayed or did not occur. Examples are included in other sections above where, often, multiple failures of management occurred.

Management of patients undergoing oesophagectomy

Key messages
• Preoperative resuscitation was often inadequate after oesophageal rupture.
• Monitoring of direct arterial pressure, central venous pressure, urine output and temperature is routine practice; in selected cases a pulmonary artery catheter may be useful.
• Anaesthetists using one lung ventilation (OLV) should ensure that they have appropriate training and experience in this technique
• Chest infection, from whatever cause, is a major precursor of sepsis and death. This is an area of potential improvement.

Written by Dr Kathy Sherry FRCA in consultation with surgical and anaesthetic advisors (see pages 10 and 11)

Hospital Episode Statistics[7] report that about 2000 oesophagectomies are performed annually in England and in the last five years the death rate has been between 9.5-10.5%. From the 1996/7 sample NCEPOD received 78 completed anaesthetic questionnaires for review. Most oesophagectomies were done "in-hours" and by senior anaesthetists.

Grade of the most senior anaesthetist (working alone)

Consultant	67	(20)
Associate specialist	1	(1)
Staff grade	3	(2)
Specialist registrar year 4	4	(2)
Specialist registrar year 3	2	(1)
Specialist registrar year 2	1	(1)

Age of patient (years)

<50	1
50 - 59	11
60 – 69	29
70 – 79	35
>79	2

Forty-three (55%) patients had concurrent disease. Twenty-nine (37%) patients had cardiac disease, five had respiratory disease and a further nine had both cardiac and respiratory disease.

Oesophageal rupture

Five patients underwent surgery for oesophageal rupture; all were in poor condition and "likely to die". These included a 65-year-old patient with an oesophageal rupture between 10 and 22 days previously who was septic, on positive pressure ventilation and receiving inotropic support, and an 85-year-old patient whose oesophagus had ruptured 15 days previously, and who was initially treated conservatively and was receiving intravenous fluids. The other three, despite their poor condition, had not received any form of resuscitation preoperatively. Two were anaemic (Hb 9.3g.dl⁻¹) and one had a Hb 17.2g.dl⁻¹, bicarbonate 17m.mol.l⁻¹, pH 7.18 and glucose 12.3m.mol.l⁻¹. Spontaneous oesophageal rupture is infrequent and its diagnosis is sometimes delayed. These patients require preoperative resuscitation in the same way as a similarly dehydrated patient with intra-abdominal perforation.

Operative monitoring

Standard operative monitoring included direct arterial pressure, central venous pressure, urine output and temperature. In 45 (58%) patients, all four variables were monitored. Direct arterial pressure was monitored in 73 (94%), CVP in 69 (88%) and urine output in 73 (94%) patients, temperature was monitored in only 51 (65%) of cases. One patient, a 74-year-old man with severe cardiac disease and anaesthetised by a specialist registrar year 4, had none of these. His trachea was extubated following surgery. His temperature was 34°C in the recovery area where he was given neostigmine, doxapram and naloxone before he was sent to the general ward. Two patients had only the direct arterial monitoring, one anaesthetised by a consultant and one by a specialist registrar year 4. Of the patients reviewed none had a pulmonary artery catheter inserted. In this group of elderly patients with a high incidence of cardiac disease and undergoing major surgery including large fluid fluxes a pulmonary artery catheter can be useful. It requires practice to insert and interpret. However, it allows a more accurate assessment of fluid loading and the facility to optimise the cardiac output.

Double lumen tube

One-lung ventilation (OLV) is associated with several well-recognised complications. Anaesthetists using this technique should ensure that they have appropriate training and experience to use this technique safely.

In 66 (86%) patients a double lumen tube was used or its placement attempted. In 30% of these cases problems were encountered. These are presented in the accompanying table.

Thirteen (20%) of the 66 patients suffered arterial desaturation at some time during one-lung ventilation; in some, high airway pressures accompanied this. The two main causes of arterial desaturation during one-lung ventilation are an incorrectly positioned double lumen tube and intrapulmonary shunting of blood.

Correct placement of a double lumen tube requires practice and is more likely to be achieved by the anaesthetists who use them regularly. For some anaesthetists, when working with a general surgeon who has a small oesophageal practice, this experience is acquired slowly. No anaesthetist reported using a fibreoptic bronchoscope to confirm the position of the tube, either before or during surgery, even when the tube was evidently incorrectly placed. The fibreoptic bronchoscope is now widely available and with practice it can aid correct placement and verify the tube position. In four out of the five cases (numbers 1-5 in the table below) when the experienced anaesthetist recognised poor positioning *before* surgery an alternative, more satisfactory, tube was used. A trainee who did not try an alternative tube managed the fifth case. *During* surgery, when it was suspected that arterial desaturation was related to the tube position, there was a reluctance to change to an alternative tube. In some cases the anaesthetist was prepared to tolerate the unsatisfactory situation.

The management of arterial desaturation due to intrapulmonary shunting forms part of the basic training in one-lung anaesthesia. The response should be to increase inspired oxygen, start non-dependent lung CPAP, differential dependent lung PEEP with non-dependent lung CPAP, intermittent lung inflation and, when these fail, resuming two-lung ventilation, finally returning to the supine position. Dependent lung PEEP alone has been shown to be of little use. Of these manoeuvres only the increase of inspired oxygen and two-lung ventilation were reported as having been used.

Whatever the cause, if arterial desaturation or inadequate ventilation occurs during anaesthesia it cannot be ignored. The immediate action to correct may need to take priority over surgical considerations and the surgery interupted.

Endoscopy is essential to the diagnosis, assessment and palliative treatment of oesophageal cancer. The lesion is typically polypoidal or ulcerating with bleeding friable mucosa. Stenotic cancers are not uncommon and may prevent the passage of even the smallest bougie. An intact mucosa at the leading edge of the stricture may give a false impression of a benign lesion; an impression which may be strengthened by a superficial biopsy of this intact mucosa. Judicious dilatation of the stricture and biopsies from within the strictured lumen, or the use of an aspirating needle and brush biopsies, prevent misdiagnosis. Fibreoptic instruments are easier and safer to use and provide better resolution. However, the size of the biopsy obtained with a fibreoptic instrument is significantly smaller than that obtained with a rigid instrument. The latter should only be employed by those with special expertise in its use. There is a distinctly higher incidence of cervical oesophageal perforation during the passage of a rigid instrument in elderly patients with marked osteophyte formation in the cervical spine. Perforation of the oesophagus is a catastrophic complication of endoscopy frequently brought about by vigorous and over-ambitious dilatation of malignant strictures. Expeditious treatment of such a perforation is vital and demands a high degree of judgement, taking into account the general condition of the patient, uncertainty about the diagnosis and the potential curability of the lesion if the diagnosis is already established. Such treatment can range from emergency resection to stenting. Endoscopic examination of the airway is indicated in all cases of middle third tumours to assess involvement and infiltration of the airway and thus the operability of the lesion. Twenty percent of patients with mid-third carcinoma have tracheobronchial invasion.[30] A barium study is complementary to endoscopy and, apart from showing the extent of the lesion, will reveal the presence of a tracheo-oesophageal fistula if such is present.

CT scanning is currently the only non-invasive method of staging the tumour, lymph node and distant organ involvement. Eccentric thickening is present in two thirds of cases and is not diagnostic. CT underestimates the length of the tumour and cannot accurately gauge the depth of mural involvement. Infiltration of adjacent mediastinal structures is more predictable and relies on the loss of the fat planes. However fat planes may be absent in cachectic and irradiated patients. Use of CT in the assessment of aortic and tracheal involvement is difficult, subjective and minimally useful in determining operability. Overall accuracy for the diagnosis of tracheobronchial invasion by CT scanning is 85% and is roughly similar to that for aortic wall invasion. However sensitivity for both is around 50%. Regional lymphadenopathy is detectable by CT scan only on the basis of lymph node enlargement but metastases from oesophageal cancer are frequently found in normal sized nodes. The accuracy of CT scanning in predicting mediastinal involvement is under 60% with a sensitivity of less than 30%. There is a much wider range of sensitivity and specificity for CT scans of abdominal lymphadenopathy. CT is particularly good at detecting adrenal, pulmonary and brain metastases. Ultrasound is more reliable in detecting hepatic metastases since isodense deposits may escape detection on CT scanning. NMR does not offer any advantages over CT in the diagnosis or staging of oesophageal carcinoma.

Endoscopic ultrasound is a promising technique for assessing the depth of penetration by tumour and adjacent organ involvement as well as lymphadenopathy. Until recently this technique was restricted to non-obstructing tumours. However design changes in the ultrasound probe have helped to partially overcome this problem. The accuracy of endoscopic ultrasound is greatest in patients with transmural tumours,[31] particularly those invading adjacent structures. Restricted availability as a consequence of high cost currently limits the use of endoscopic ultrasound.

A significant number of patients with oesophageal carcinoma are elderly and frail, with a history of alcohol and tobacco abuse, and a high incidence of cardiovascular and respiratory disease. It must not be forgotten that patients may be in a poor nutritional state solely due to starvation and that this can occur even with a relatively small, curable tumour. Improvement of nutritional status prior to surgery is helpful. Patients in respiratory failure are not surgical candidates. Neither are those with cardiac failure due to extensive cardiac infarction. Patients with ejection fractions of less than 40% tolerate radical resections poorly. Patients with severe angina or tight aortic stenosis with preserved left ventricular function can undergo coronary bypass surgery or valve replacement four weeks prior to oesophageal surgery providing they are relatively fit and free of metastases.

No patient with an active chest infection should be submitted to surgery until antibiotic therapy and physiotherapy have cleared the infection. Patients with an FEV1 of less than one litre are unlikely to survive or benefit from a radical oesophageal resection as the interstitial oedema resulting from disruption of the pulmonary lymphatics, especially in those with a low serum albumin, further compromises a precarious respiratory status. Rarely should a patient aged 80 or over be subjected to radical resection in view of the steep rise in mortality with extremes of age.

No patient who is unfit to withstand a major surgical assault should be subjected to radical surgery and no surgeon with inadequate training (in all aspects of oesophageal surgery including preoperative assessment, intraoperative management and postoperative care) should undertake the care of such patients independently. A well conducted, patient-tailored operation supported by skilled anaesthesia, including invasive monitoring of haemodynamic and respiratory parameters, will produce a better outcome for patients undergoing major oesophageal resections.

Further reading

Ellis HJF et al. *Oesophagogastrectomy for carcinoma of the oesophagus and cardia.* Journal of Thoracic and Cardiovascular Surgery. 1997; **113**:836-848

Proposed facilities for the specialist practice of oesophageal surgery

> **Key messages**
>
> - A multidisciplinary team within a specialist centre should manage patients with oesophageal disease.

Personal commentary written by Mr S Michael Griffin MD, FRCS

Introduction

The majority of the workload and use of resources in a department of oesophageal surgery will be in the management of oesophago-gastric cancer. A multidisciplinary team within a specialist centre providing all investigative and treatment modalities must manage patients with oesophageal cancer. The concentration of cases within such a unit would allow accurate audit of outcome and ensure appropriate recruitment to clinical trials. Such a unit would be sited within a cancer centre.

Multi-disciplinary team

The core members of the multidisciplinary team dealing with oesophageal conditions include:

- oesophago-gastric surgeons including thoracic surgeons with expertise in oesophageal surgery
- specialist oesophageal anaesthetists
- diagnostic and interventional radiologists
- clinical and medical oncologists
- specialised upper GI histopathologist
- upper GI nurse specialist and database manager
- palliative care specialist

Other members who are key to providing this service but not core staff include:

- specialist intensivist with experience in management of patients following oesophageal surgery
- medical gastroenterologist
- General Practitioner
- nutritionist
- dedicated physiotherapist

The specialist centre would comprise expertise and specialisation as outlined above.

All investigative modalities must be available. These include:

- video endoscopy
- pulmonary physiology laboratory
- oesophageal physiology laboratory
- computerised tomography (ideally spiral)
- endoluminal ultrasound

The specialist centre would require adequate inpatient facilities in terms of beds on a ward with specialist nurses, theatre time and experienced anaesthesia with ready access to intensive care and high dependency units.

Full back up with an identified interventional radiologist with suitable imaging including access to spiral CT on a 24-hour basis.

Surgeons practising in the centre must have specialist expertise in the field of oesophageal cancer. Surgeons should work in teams of at least two and preferably four to ensure continuity of care and to provide a consultant-based service throughout the year. These surgeons would devote all their fixed sessions to gastro-oesophageal surgery, which would include a service for benign diseases.

Upper GI nurse specialists would act as a focus for the patients referred to the centre and as a contact point in times of difficulty or anxiety. These nurse specialists would help to coordinate therapy, to liaise with all members of the team and to direct the collation of data for regular audit. Dietary problems occur in almost all patients postoperatively, especially whilst undergoing neo-adjuvant therapy. The upper GI nurse specialist and dietician are essential to diagnose these feeding problems and treat them early. The upper GI nurse specialist would form a vital link in primary care and would visit patients in the postoperative and post-therapeutic period.

The multi-disciplinary team would meet on a weekly basis to discuss all cases and to formulate management plans.

Most patients would present to smaller units where the diagnosis will be made. Protocols could be disseminated to ensure similar standards of diagnosis and urgent referral. All potentially curable oesophageal cancer patients should be referred to specialist centres. Upper GI surgeons working single-handed should not continue. They should be encouraged to be part of the central team with sessions in a specialist unit performing surgery. For maximum efficiency over 250 new cases of oesophago-gastric cancer should be assessed in such a centre. This would serve a population of at least one million.

Better investigative facilities and centralisation of surgical expertise would result in better preoperative assessment to enable patients to avoid unnecessary surgery and receive all appropriate treatment for their general health and the stage of their disease. Many more patients with T2 and T3 tumours will be considered for neo-adjuvant chemo-radiotherapy. These patients would be included in clinical trials. There is much evidence to support the role of the multidisciplinary team and the specialist centre in the management of oesophageal disease. Oesophago-gastric surgery carries the highest postoperative mortality of any elective surgery. A recent survey of the world literature[32] showed an average mortality of 15%. Audited results from specialist centres in the United Kingdom have brought mortality figures down to below 5% despite the treatment of high risk patients.[33] In specialist centres the five-year survival figures for patients undergoing curative surgery for cancer is in the region of 25-30%, similar to the best figures in the world. Overall survival in the United Kingdom is well below this figure.

The complications of oesophageal surgery are significant. Over 30% of patients suffer major complications following thoraco-abdominal surgery. Consultant input and access on site to interventional radiology on a 24-hour basis is essential to treat these complications. A high level of manpower and expertise is essential to manage these patients effectively. This can only be achieved in a specialist centre with at least two and preferably four surgeons and two interventional radiologists.

The stage of the disease and its assessment preoperatively are crucially important in the management of oesophageal cancer. Spiral CT and endoluminal ultrasound are pivotal to this accurate assessment. These modalities are relatively expensive and endoluminal ultrasound is only available in a few large centres. Resources need to be concentrated in specialist centres so that there is no duplication resulting in financial wastage.

Multi-modality therapy, particularly including neo-adjuvant chemo-radiotherapy may well improve outcome in operative patients. The cost of radiotherapy equipment restricts this service to cancer centres where the specialist centre should be based. Furthermore the use of expensive palliative measures in those patients with oesophageal cancer not suitable for curative surgery should be concentrated in these centres and not distributed in smaller hospitals resulting in duplication of expensive equipment.

Setting up such centres would prevent the occasional surgeon performing less than five cases of oesophageal surgery or resections per year. Although specialist centres always raise the spectre of increased cost there would be potential savings by concentrating expensive equipment (spiral CT and endoscopic ultrasound) and resources (intensive care and high dependency units) on fewer sites. There would be a reduction in operative mortality. In addition the early recognition of complications and their treatment would reduce ICU stay and prevent a later transfer to a specialist unit with associated prolonged stay.

Oesophageal stenting

Key messages

- Surgeons, endoscopists and interventional radiologists may be involved in procedures to insert oesophageal stents. They should all be aware of the indications, risks and overall management of patients requiring this procedure.
- Patients should receive detailed information about life with a stent.

Personal commentary written by Mr Simon Raimes MD FRCS

There are now a variety of oesophageal prostheses that require different techniques of insertion. Surgeons, endoscopists and interventional radiologists may be involved individually or as teams in procedures to insert stents and should equally be aware of the indications, risks and overall management of the patient if mortality is to be minimised.

The primary indication for oesophageal stent insertion is relief of malignant dysphagia in patients who are unsuitable for, or have failed, other techniques to improve their swallowing. It is presently not regarded as first-line treatment except in very elderly or unfit patients. None of the presently available stents consistently allow completely normal swallowing and should not be used unless there is significant unrelieved dysphagia except in two circumstances. The first is in the treatment of an aero-digestive fistula involving the oesophagus and the other is the rare situation where there is uncontrolled blood loss from an oesophageal cancer.

Oesophageal stent insertion is a palliative procedure in patients expected to have a limited life span. It does not affect the natural history of the underlying disease although the resulting better nutrition and morale of the patient may improve survival. It is not a treatment for a patient in the last phase of a terminal illness where other palliative measures are more appropriate.

There are presently two types of stent in common use. Stents inserted at open operation are now only very rarely indicated. Rigid reinforced tube stents are inserted endoscopically using a pulsion technique. The newer self-expandable covered stents are inserted either endoscopically or under radiological control alone. Randomised trials are being conducted to determine the possible advantages of the self-expandable stents since they are five to six times more expensive to purchase. Whichever stent is used the procedure should be regarded as an operation and the patient and their relatives fully informed of the risks and likely benefits of the procedure. It is still not certain whether the significant mortality of rigid stent insertion is avoided by use of the self-expandable stents. High standards of care before, during and after the procedure are required to minimise the mortality.

Preoperative preparation should include correction of dehydration and electrolyte disturbances. Patients with complete dysphagia are usually significantly malnourished and often have chronic or acute aspiration into the respiratory tract. Antibiotics and chest physiotherapy are essential in preparing the patient with any evidence of infection.

Stenting should be performed under heavy intravenous sedation with a short-acting benzodiazepine combined with a short-acting opiate. There is no indication for the use of general anaesthesia but it is sensible for an anaesthetist to administer the sedation to these very sick patients. The heavily sedated patient must receive oxygen, have monitoring of oxygen saturation and ECG and have their airway cared for and protected until fully awake. Insertion of the stent and pre-dilatation, if required, must be performed under radiological control.

Many patients experience chest pain after stent insertion and may require strong analgesia for up to 72 hours. Oesophageal perforation during insertion is a recognised risk of these procedures and if suspected should be confirmed by clinical examination, an erect chest X-ray film and possibly a water-soluble contrast swallow. In most cases the tube will occlude the leak, but a short course of intravenous broad-spectrum antibiotics is advisable. If the clinical signs deteriorate or the leak is uncontained then a decision on further management has to be made in light of the overall condition of the patient. Stents that cross the gastro-oesophageal junction can produce significant problems. Uncontrolled reflux is a frequent problem and the recovering patient must be nursed in the sitting position to prevent aspiration. In the longer term prescription of an antisecretory drug and a prokinetic agent are important to decrease oesophageal damage and chronic aspiration. Stents in this position may impact on the greater curve of the stomach resulting in an ongoing inability to eat that can be very difficult to solve.

Patients should receive detailed information about life with a stent. They will also need expert dietetic advice. The patient and their family should be offered contact with appropriate cancer support services in view of the poor prognosis.

Further reading

Blazely JM, Alderson D. *Palliative treatments of carcinoma of the oesophagus and stomach.* In:Upper Gastrointestinal Surgery, eds. Griffin SM, Raimes SA. W B Saunders, London 1997 pp 213-244.

Sturgess RP, Morris AI. *Metal stents in the oesophagus.* Gut 1995; 37: 593-594.

Spinal surgery

Written by Mr Ron Hoile MS, FRCS in consultation with the spinal surgery advisors (see page 11)

List of procedures

Benign disease

Procedure (may be multiple for individual patients)	Number
Decompressive cervical surgery with or without fusion/stabilisation	14
Decompressive lumbar surgery with or without fusion/stabilisation	9
Cervical fusion for fracture/dislocation and/or instability (all levels)	8
Application of halo traction vest	4
Transoral odontoidectomy	2
Debridement of thoracolumbar vertebrae for osteomyelitis (pyogenic 1, tuberculous 1)	2
Decompression of thoracic epidural abscess	2
Revision of cervical spinal fusion	2
Fixation of thoracolumbar spinal fractures with or without cord injury	2
Miscellaneous: (one each of – revision of scoliosis surgery/removal of rods, cervical microdiscectomy, decompressive thoracic surgery, debridement of wound, tracheostomy)	5

Metastatic malignant disease

Procedure (may be multiple for individual patients)	Number
Decompressive thoracic surgery with or without fusion/stabilisation	13
Decompressive cervical surgery with or without fusion/stabilisation	7
Decompressive lumbar surgery with or without fusion/stabilisation	6
Biopsy of lumbar vertebral body	1

Total number of patients = 76

Urology

Key messages

- Team assessment is required for all elderly patients, particularly when contemplating radical surgery for malignant disease, because of the high incidence of other medical problems.
- A balance has to be maintained between too aggressive surgery and the quality of life when carrying out surgery in the presence of metastases or following previous radiotherapy.
- In urology there was a high involvement of Consultants.

Written by Mr Ron Hoile MS, FRCS and Emeritus Professor Vic Tindall FRCOG in consultation with the urology advisors (see page 12)

List of procedures

Procedure (may be multiple for individual patients)	Number
Transurethral resection of prostate (benign and malignant)	106
Cystoscopy (+/- biopsy)	96
Transurethral resection of bladder tumour	80
Nephrectomy (malignant and benign)	45
Testicular & scrotal procedures	25
Ureteric stenting	18
Cystectomy	16
Ileal conduit	14
Other procedures on bladder (e.g. repair of rupture/perforation)	13
Bladder neck incision	12
Open prostatic procedures	12
Miscellaneous ureteric procedures (e.g. reimplantation, ureterolysis etc.)	8
Procedures for ureteric/bladder calculus	8
Miscellaneous renal procedures (e.g. re-exploration for bleeding, removal of packs, nephrostomy)	7
Urethra dilatation	7
Miscellaneous urethra procedures e.g. drainage of periurethral abscess)	7
Evacuation of bladder clots	6
Cystodiathermy	6
Combined transurethral resection of prostate and bladder tumour	5
Penile procedures	4
Laparotomy	4
Percutaneous nephrolithotomy	4
Resuture of wound	2
Repair inguinal hernia	2
Right hemicolectomy	2
Total abdominal hysterectomy	2
Transverse colostomy	2
Miscellaneous (one each of: cholecystectomy, splenectomy, hemiarthroplasty, manual evacuation of faeces, excision retroperitoneal nodes, pelvic exenteration)	6

Total number of patients = 518

Review of cases

In many of the cases reviewed the patients had died of progressive disease and the urological intervention seemed to be part of the overall care of the patient, with death occurring perhaps a week or two after surgery. Most deaths occurred in patients undergoing surgery for cancer; it is gratifying to see how few deaths resulted from the management of patients with septic stone disease or conditions such as female urinary incontinence or benign prostatic enlargement in men. There was also a high involvement of senior surgeons. In 92% of the 518 cases reviewed the consultant was involved in the preoperative decision making. Consultants were present in theatre in 79% of all cases and in 71% of cases were the principal operators.

Elderly patients

The majority of the deaths were in elderly patients; 77% (399/518) were aged 70 and over, of whom 46% (184/399) were aged 80 and over.

Comorbidity

Co-existing problems were present in 87% (449/518) of the patients and there were two or more problems in 60% (271/449) of these patients. Nevertheless death was not anticipated or expected (by the surgeons) in 42% (219/518) of the cases.

Postmortem examinations

There were several cases in which it was considered that a postmortem examination should have been performed and there was no real explanation as to why this was not recommended.

Recognised hazards

Haemorrhage is a recognised risk of nephrectomy and/or difficult major surgery and was the major factor in five deaths.

Pulmonary embolism was the cause of death in only 1% (7/518) of the cases reviewed.

Inappropriate surgery or management

There were nine deaths in which the advisors considered that the surgery for the particular patient was inappropriate. Often it was inadequate preoperative assessment which led to inappropriate surgery, for example proper assessment and CT scanning might have prevented surgery in four of the cases detailed below. Major urological cancer surgery in patients with an ASA classification of 3 or more may be technically feasible from a surgical point of view but, as in the cases presented below, is sometimes not tolerated by the patient. In such cases less aggressive surgery and an early referral for palliative care assessment would seem to represent a better management choice. Criticism of these nine cases, where it was agreed that surgery was generally inappropriate, should not be seen out of context. They represent a small percentage (2%, 9/518) of the cases studied and (although NCEPOD does not have the denominator data) an even smaller percentage of urological surgery in general.

Age and sex	ASA grade	Procedure	Comments by the advisors
62F	3	Total cystectomy	Invasive TCC. Advised cystectomy despite being hypertensive and was on warfarin because of previous aortic valve replacement. Previous CVA. Postoperative persistent hypertension and overwhelming sepsis. Considered to be an inappropriate operation.
70M	3	Nephrectomy, cystectomy and ileal conduit	Anaplastic tumour of kidney infiltrating perirenal tissues. Palliative care was considered to be more appropriate.
71M	4	Initial operation was radical left nephrectomy. Final operation was laparotomy for bleeding from body of pancreas	This man had a stable bronchogenic cancer. A left adrenal mass involving the kidney, aorta and coeliac axis was detected. Delayed haemorrhage and CVA followed an inappropriate radical operation in this high-risk patient.
71F	3	Cystectomy and ileal neo-bladder	A poor choice of operation in view of the extensive disease present and ASA grade.
72M	4	Total cystectomy	Salvage cystectomy post irradiation. Postoperative haemorrhage and subsequent sepsis. Were the risks of this type of surgery justified?
74F	3	Total cystectomy and ileal loop diversion	Reason for the procedure in the presence of lung metastases not clear. An operative blood loss of three litres was related to her gross obesity.
74M	4	Cystoscopy	Poor risk with COPD. Inappropriate cystoscopy in the presence of known metastatic disease and the absence of symptoms.
76F	3	Right hemicolectomy, total cystectomy, hysterectomy and ileal conduit	Inappropriate radical urological surgery was carried out by a general surgeon with an interest in gastroenterology when a partial cystectomy was all the urological surgery necessary in the management of a caecal carcinoma involving the dome of the bladder.
84M	3	Radical nephrectomy	High medical risk – previous MI and DVT; inpatient for three weeks prior to operation. No anticoagulant prophylaxis. Locum consultant surgeon. Postmortem examination revealed lung metastases and massive pulmonary embolism. Considered poor case assessment.

Minor problems

The preoperative assessment or work-up was thought to be less than ideal in two cases and in one of these cases the postmortem examination revealed an undetected carcinoma of the bladder and secondary lung metastases. The other patient was considered to be unsuitable for the day case surgery which was done in view of known morbid obesity and previous major anaesthetic problems. Did the unit in question have a protocol for the selection of patients suitable for day case surgery?

Postoperative problems

The postoperative care was identified to be of poor quality in eight cases (fluid overload in two, sepsis in two cases and poor continuity of care by general medical team in four cases).

The problem of patients being on general surgical or medical wards *without the speciality trained nurses* was considered a factor which influenced the outcome in several of these cases. One patient, for example, who was unable to be put on ICU after a pelvic exenteration, was admitted to a medical CCU and subsequently died from intravenous fluid overload. NCEPOD has commented on similar points in a previous report.[48]

Central venous pressure monitoring during anaesthesia and surgery

Key messages
• CVP monitoring may be indicated for patients with acute or chronic medical conditions.
• Equipment for CVP monitoring should be available in operating theatres in which major surgery is performed.
• CVP insertion is a core anaesthetic skill that needs regular practice.

Personal commentary written by Dr Roop Kishen FRCA

Anaesthesia and surgery have undergone great changes in the last two decades. Major and increasingly more complex surgery is being undertaken in physiologically compromised patients who present for surgery with co-morbidity, especially respiratory and cardiac disease (reference 49, page 41). In some of these patients surgery would not have been contemplated but for several important developments which enhance patient safety. These include the use of appropriate and timely monitoring and the support services of intensive care and high dependency units. For routine and emergency surgery minimal monitoring standards have been established. However, in many situations the safe conduct of anaesthesia and surgery requires additional, more invasive monitoring such as central venous pressure (CVP), intra-arterial blood pressure and pulmonary arterial catheterisation.

Equipment

The equipment for insertion and monitoring of CVP and suitably trained assistants should be available in all operating theatres.

Training

CVP monitoring is easy to learn and teach. Anaesthetists learn CVP line insertion during their basic training and all should be familiar with the technique. However, it is an acquired skill and, to be proficient, it has to be practised. With practice CVP line insertion is not time consuming, it can be placed easily and has few complications providing well known basic rules are followed. In anaesthetised ventilated patients the internal jugular is preferable to the subclavian route, it is associated with fewer complications e.g. pneumothorax and concealed haemorrhage. However, if the internal jugular vein cannot be accessed, the subclavian route can be used providing the benefits of monitoring outweigh the risks of complications.

Patient selection

Some types of surgery are associated with the use of CVP routinely. CVP monitoring is well established for cardiac surgery. Most anaesthetists will use invasive monitoring during major vascular surgery, e.g. aortic aneurysm repair (reference 49, page 68). NCEPOD 1993/1994[49] reported that 79 out of 85 patients undergoing emergency aortic aneurysm repair had a CVP line inserted for monitoring purposes. The report goes on to say that "the role of invasive monitoring is undisputed; central venous and arterial pressures are recognised to be valuable aids to safe management of patients during and after these operations".

In other patients who are undergoing anaesthesia and surgery, however major, routine use of CVP monitoring is not yet established (reference 49, page 79). The reasons for this are not clear. It is possible that the small risks of CVP catheter insertion, when balanced against its benefits are not fully appreciated. All anaesthetists recognise the importance of minimal monitoring of patients during anaesthesia and surgery. CVP monitoring, in selected cases and for patients at risk, should be regarded as an extension of this monitoring.

Which patients would benefit from CVP monitoring?

Surgical indications include major thoracic surgery (e.g. oesophagectomy), major abdominal surgery (massive resections, major liver surgery, pelvic clearance etc.), surgery for complex fistulae, resection of phaeochromocytoma, major orthopaedic reconstruction, major plastic and burns surgery, sepsis, trauma etc. - all cases in which large fluid shifts, major blood losses or circulatory instability are expected during their surgery and postoperative course.

A group of patients which appear to the advisors less readily recognised are those with acute or chronic medical conditions that may compromise their tolerance of blood loss and fluid infusions. Examples of these include patients with a history of cardiac failure, those at risk of developing postoperative acute renal failure, patients with dialysis dependent chronic renal failure etc. This list is not exhaustive; any patient at risk is a candidate for CVP monitoring.

Age itself is a relative indication. As longevity increases, more and more elderly patients will present for surgery. This population is physiologically less competent and has many co-morbidities including ischaemic heart disease, hypertension (increasingly treated with potent ACE inhibitors), diabetes and poor renal function. For safe conduct of anaesthesia and surgery, for appropriate fluid management and timely cardiovascular support in these patients, CVP monitoring should be considered as routine as other standard monitoring. It is accepted that insertion of a CVP line does not guarantee outcome. However, its use in this population should make their management easier and more logical. This in itself may avoid mortality and morbidity.

In many patients with severe preoperative dehydration or sepsis requiring resuscitation, CVP monitoring is a useful guide to the effectiveness of therapy.

Interpretation of the CVP

In its interpretation, CVP monitoring requires understanding and experience. It must be appreciated that CVP monitoring is not a substitute for the measurement of cardiac output. CVP measurement does not equate with blood volume or left ventricular function. It does not tell us about the right ventricular function either! CVP monitoring is an indirect measure of right heart preload and it indicates the ability of a particular patient to deal with the infused fluid load. In certain circumstances it may also indicate the need for inotropic support. Thus it can aid fluid management in many patients, especially those at risk. NCEPOD has repeatedly pointed out the dangers of inappropriate fluid infusions in 'at risk' patients. In such patients it is possible to avoid large, inappropriate fluid infusions and either provide inotropic support or institute further investigative monitoring such as pulmonary artery catheter or oesophageal Doppler.

Patients undergoing surgery and general anaesthesia without CVP monitoring.

In these patients, amongst many others, the advisors questioned whether CVP monitoring might have been useful.

Age	ASA	Operation	Co-morbidity	Outcome
73	3	Radical hysterectomy and node dissection	Previous MI, angina, COPD, heavy smoker, three previous CVAs)	Per- and post-operative hypotension. Returned to the ward. Developed pulmonary oedema
91	3	TAH, bilateral salpingo-oophorectomy	Frail	Returned to the ward. Very positive fluid balance. Developed cardiac and renal failure
90	4	De-bulk ovarian tumour adherent to bowel	Two previous MIs, CCF, COPD, asthma, ascites, SOB at rest	Per- and post-operative hypotension. Returned to ICU/HDU
57	4	Bilateral oophorectomy and omentectomy	44kg, cachectic, ascites, SpO_2 84%	CVP inserted postoperatively for feeding. Desaturation in recovery. Returned to the ward
83	5	Ovarian mass excision, colostomy, omentectomy	Bowel obstruction, 'moribund'	Returned to the ward
84	3	TAH, bilateral salpingo-oophorectomy, omentectomy and right hemicolectomy	Mild CCF and AF	Peroperative hypotension, SAP 80mmHg for two hours. Fast AF in recovery. Returned to the ward
78	3	Laparoscopic mobilisation of the colon failed, progressed to colon excision via Pfannenstiel incision, nephrectomy via subcostal incision.	IHD, CCF, AF, orthopnoea with five pillows	Five hours of surgery. Epidural top-up at the end of the operation. In recovery hypotension, cardiac arrest and died
70	3	Total gastrectomy and splenectomy	Hypertension, AF, IHD	Epidural top-ups at the beginning and end of surgery. Prolonged episodes of hypotension peroperatively. Returned to the ward
76	5	Acute abdomen. Attempted bowel resection	Unwell, on steroids and NSAIDs for vascular and musculoskeletal problems. K^+ 5.5mmol.L^{-1}, Cr 185micro mol.L^{-1}, U 20.9mmol.L^{-1}	No preoperative fluids. Per-operatively; fluids 1500ml, BP 80/35, pulse 120. Returned to ICU, died 6h later
59	4	Laparotomy, bilateral ureterolysis	Obese, pneumoconiosis, cor pulmonale, unstable angina, CCF, renal failure	Returned to ICU, then the ward. Developed ischaemic colon, probably embolic

Admission on the day of surgery

> ## Key messages
>
> - The selection of patients for admission on the day of surgery should conform to locally agreed guidelines.
> - Patients should be fully assessed and investigated at an outpatient visit preoperatively.
> - Some patients need joint decisions between specialists, in particular between consultant surgeons and consultant anaesthetists.
> - The timing of admission on the day of surgery should allow a final clinical assessment by both surgeon and anaesthetist before the patient enters the theatre complex.

Written by Dr Kathy Sherry FRCA in consultation with the anaesthetic advisors (see page 10)

In this sample of deaths, 77 anaesthetic questionnaires were received, relating to patients who had undergone scheduled or elective surgery and who were also admitted on the day of operation. They were not scheduled for day case surgery.

Classification of final operation*/ASA grade

	ASA 1	ASA 2	ASA 3	ASA 4	ASA 5	Total
Scheduled	-	14	16	6	-	36
Elective	4	18	17	2	-	41
Total	**4**	**32**	**33**	**8**	-	77

* see glossary for classification and ASA grades

The two elective ASA 4 patients were a 64-year-old man, for a transurethral resection of prostate, who had angina on minimal exertion and at rest, and an 85-year-old man for palliative oesophagoscopy and dilatation.

Age of patient (years)

30 - 39	1
40 - 49	2
50 - 59	3
60 - 69	17
70 -79	31
80 -89	20
90 - 99	3
Total	**77**

The following seven patients had *no* preoperative investigations.

Age (years)	Operation	General/local anaesthesia	Medical disorder
91	Cataract removal	Local	None
92	Ectropion repair	General	'Frail'
74	Urethral dilatation	General	None
70	Check cystoscopy	General	Asthma
68	Check cystoscopy	General	COPD and peripheral vascular disease
78	Laparoscopic inguinal hernia repair	General	Angina
65	Palliative oesophagoscopy and dilatation	General	Recurrent ascites

Twenty-one cases are presented in outline to illustrate the range of cases that were reviewed. NCEPOD is not commenting on the suitability of individual cases for admission on the day of surgery but hopes that their presentation here may stimulate useful local debate.

Age	ASA	Classification	Medical problems	Operation
68	3	Scheduled	COPD and peripheral vascular disease*	Check cystoscopy
64	4	Elective	Angina on minimal exertion and at rest	TURP
77	3	Scheduled	Ischaemic heart disease	TAH and bilateral salpingo-oophorectomy
76	4	Scheduled	Ischaemic heart disease, CVA, alcoholism	EUA larynx, pharynx and oesophagus
78	3	Elective	Angina, obesity (90Kg)*	Laparoscopic inguinal hernia repair
67	2	Scheduled	IHD	Thoraco-abdominal oesophagectomy
72	2	Elective	IHD and hypertension, no preoperative CXR, died of thoracic aortic dissection	Vaginal hysterectomy and anterior vaginal repair
88	3	Elective	IHD	TURP
88	2	Elective	'Frail', preoperative ECG only	TURBT
56	3	Elective	Diabetes, angina on minimal exertion and at rest	Colposuspension
76	3	Elective	Angina	TURP
85	3	Scheduled	No preoperative ECG	TURBT
70	3	Elective	Severe angina	Percutaneous nephrolithotomy
81	2	Scheduled	No preoperative ECG, MI 36hr postoperatively	Retropubic prostatectomy
83	4	Scheduled	Severe ischaemic heart disease	TURBT
60	3	Elective	Unstable NIDDM, IHD	Cystoscopy
70	3	Elective	IHD	Total gastrectomy and splenectomy
68	3	Elective	Renal impairment and NIDDM	TURBT
80	2	Elective	IDDM, angina, dementia, admitted one hour preoperatively	Vitrectomy
59	2	Elective	History of difficult previous anaesthetic, obese (115kg), smoked 30/day, hiatus hernia	Check cystoscopy
40	2	Elective	Down's syndrome, mitral regurgitation, no preoperative ECG	Laparoscopic cholecystectomy

* Patient had no preoperative investigations, and is also featured in the previous table.

In a drive to reduce length of hospital stay and increase patient throughput many patients are being admitted on the day of surgery. We do need to recognise that for some patients admission on the day of surgery is not in their best interest.

A large number of the deaths following scheduled or elective surgery were unanticipated. The impact of an unexpected death in the family cannot be measured but it is unlikely to be eased by precipitate admission for a planned operation.

Patients admitted on the day of surgery require meticulous pre-admission preoperative assessment and preparation.

Guidelines on patient suitability, locally agreed between the surgical and anaesthetic staff, should be encouraged.

Preoperative assessment

Assessment should be at a dedicated outpatient clinic allowing time for review of investigations before admission as well as co-ordination of the admission, referral for specialist opinions or special investigations, as required. At this time preoperative preparation including the management of routine medication should be explained and supported by written instruction.

Junior surgical staff often run assessment clinics. However, some individuals will need referral to and assessment by an anaesthetist before admission.

There are no absolute criteria for suitability; assessment should consider the following:

Medical status
Age alone should be considered but is not a contraindication; poor physiological status is. Patients who are healthy or have stable medical conditions are more likely to be suitable. Patients with unstable medical conditions need more careful consideration.

Examination of the table above shows a striking incidence of ischaemic heart disease that was known of or detectable preoperatively. Patients are often anxious about hospital admission and their impending anaesthesia and surgery. It is recognised that myocardial ischaemia is worsened by stress and that preoperative myocardial ischaemia is associated with increased postoperative death. It should be questioned, therefore, whether patients with ischaemic heart disease are suitable for admission on the day of surgery.

Operation
The type of operation alone is not a contraindication. For example, a young, healthy individual having a major operation may be considered suitable for admission on the day of surgery; a patient with an unstable medical condition having a minor operation is likely to be unsuitable. Patients undergoing palliative surgery should be assessed individually.

Social factors
Social circumstances need to be considered. It may be difficult for the patient to get to hospital on time and in a suitably prepared emotional state. Admission on the day of surgery may cause unacceptable anxiety for the patient or their carer.

The anaesthesia and surgery may be by medical staff unfamiliar with the patient or there may have been a change in the patients' condition between preoperative assessment and admission. It is important therefore, that admission on the day of surgery should be timed to allow the surgical and anaesthetic staff to make a final clinical assessment *before* the patient enters the theatre complex.

Complications associated with postoperative analgesia

Written by Dr Kathy Sherry FRCA

Twelve questionnaires reported complications with postoperative analgesia.

Age	Operation	Analgesia	Location and problem	Intervention
50	L4/5 spinal fusion.	Intravenous bolus opiate in recovery.	In recovery area, acute laryngeal oedema in response to morphine	Died from the complication
81	Tracheostomy and EUA larynx	Intravenous bolus opiate in recovery, subcutaneous opiate on the ward	In recovery area, transient hypoventilation	Doxapram given, resolved
83	Left nephrectomy	Continuous intravenous opioid	In recovery area, drowsy	Responded to naloxone. Already scheduled for ICU
76	Laparotomy for bleeding gastric ulcer.	Continuous infusion of opiate	In HDU, opiate narcosis	Changed to Tramadol
83	Total abdominal hysterectomy and high anterior resection.	Opiate PCA with background infusion	In HDU, "relative opiate overdose"	No treatment
81	Bilateral oophorectomy and hysterectomy.	Opiate PCA	On the ward, patient unable to use it	Changed to a continuous infusion of opiate
70	Laparotomy and over-sew bleeding duodenal ulcer	Opiate PCA	On the ward, over-sedation resulting from the patient's relatives' inappropriate use.	None
68	Open pyelonephro-lithotomy.	Opiate PCA	On the ward, at 21.00 hrs respiratory rate 6/min. and pinpoint pupils.	Responded to naloxone
83	Left nephrectomy	Opiate PCA	On the ward, drowsiness.	Responded to naloxone
70	Posterior thoracic spinal decompression and fusion following a previous anterior decompression and chest drain.	Epidural opiate	Peroperatively the epidural catheter was inserted under direct vision. The patient had infection in the chest drain site. Postoperatively he developed a paraspinal abscess.	None, developed paraplegia
72	Total gastrectomy	Epidural opiate and bupivacaine	Postoperatively on the ward he had breakthrough pain; necrosis of the distal oesophagus was not recognised.	None, patient developed sepsis and respiratory failure
54	Oesophagogastrectomy	Epidural opiate and bupivacaine	Postoperatively developed infarct of the posterior cord and paraplegia.	None

Lessons from the above patients are clear.

It is the responsibility of the anaesthetist to ensure that patients are nursed in an area where both the nursing and medical staff with primary responsibility for the patient have been appropriately trained in the analgesic techniques and are aware of the associated complications and their management.

With epidural analgesia a surgical complication causing breakthrough pain should not be missed.

Respiratory depression can occur with PCA or intravenous opioid analgesia and patients need documented monitoring according to the local protocol.

Two of the complications that were reported -laryngeal oedema following intravenous morphine and cord infarct associated with epidural analgesia - are thankfully very rare.

Non-steroidal anti-inflammatory drugs

Key messages

Non-steroidal anti-inflammatory drugs (NSAIDs) can be very useful analgesics in the perioperative period. However they should be used with caution in patients with:

- renal impairment
- hypertension and cardiac failure
- GI ulceration and bleeding
- asthma

Written by Dr Anthony Gray FRCA in consultation with the anaesthetic advisors (see page 10)

Current thinking is that if a therapy is effective it should be applied in every situation where the patient should benefit; conversely, the therapy should not be used when there are contra-indications or the risks are too great. Wherever possible, decisions on effectiveness, risks and contra-indications should be based on published evidence and guidelines. The Royal College of Anaesthetists[50] has issued "Guidelines for the Use of Non-steroidal Anti-inflammatory Drugs in the Perioperative Period". These show that NSAIDs are excellent analgesics in the right circumstances.

The questionnaires returned to NCEPOD give an insight into the way that NSAIDs are used particularly by anaesthetists.

NSAIDs were prescribed for postoperative pain for 178 patients out of the total of 1269 (14.0%). NSAIDs were prescribed in combination with IM analgesics (64 patients), PCA (28 patients) and epidural infusions (12 patients). NCEPOD did not ask for copies of prescription charts so it is not possible to say how often these drugs were actually dispensed. These figures indicate that anaesthetists are cautious about prescribing NSAIDs in the cohort of surgical patients examined in this survey, despite their undoubted efficacy in the treatment of postoperative pain.

On the other hand, many patients were prescribed NSAIDs in situations where there was the potential to precipitate adverse effects. The anaesthetic advisors agreed that such a decision was justified when NSAIDs were prescribed as part of palliative care; obviously in such situations, a further deterioration in a patient's general condition may be less important compared to achieving good control of pain. In other cases the advisors questioned their use.

The following patients, whose condition was not regarded as terminal, were prescribed NSAIDs

Age	Operation	Clinical details
78	TURP	Hypertensive, chronic renal failure with a creatinine of 500 μmol/L. On hydralazine, atenolol and bendrofluazide.
81	EUA, hysteroscopy	BP 205/110 mm Hg, no treatment. No preoperative urea or electrolyte measurement.
84	TURP	Noted preoperatively to have "*severe chronic active gastritis and ulceration*". Given diclofenac during his operation.

(continued overleaf)

Age	Operation	Clinical details
74	Laparotomy for postoperative bleeding	Preoperative renal impairment, creatinine 296 μmol/L.
74	Laparoscopic liver biopsy	Hepato-renal syndrome, creatinine 142 μmol/L, bilirubin 87.
60	Abdominal hysterectomy	Asthmatic, on beclomethasone, salbutamol and aminophylline, no known allergies. Died from acute gastric dilatation.
87	Nephrectomy	CCF, pleural effusions, NIDDM, on frusemide and amiloride. Creatinine 97μmol/L, urea 12.9 mmol/L.
76	Incision and drainage knee abscess	Septic arthritis, chronic renal failure, IHD, liver dysfunction with INR of 2.2.
70	Total gastrectomy	Hypertensive, IHD on oxprenolol. Developed oliguria day after surgery, died the following day in acute LVF.
79	Nephrectomy	Diet-controlled diabetes, anaemia.
88	ORIF cervical spine	Frail. AF. Na 123 mmol/L preoperatively. Hypotensive intra-operatively, given 5000 ml of fluid in first 24 hours. No CVP. No record of blood loss.
39	L5/S1 discectomy	Diclofenac and PCA postoperatively. Fluctuating nausea and vomiting, then collapsed eight days after surgery and could not be resuscitated. Postmortem examination showed a small colonic perforation.
83	TURP	Old MI, angina. Hypotensive during GA, given 1500 ml fluid intra-operatively over 30 minutes.
81	Incision and drainage infected hydrocoele	Poor renal function which deteriorated postoperatively
86	Division of adhesions, formation of colostomy	Two previous myocardial infarctions, AF, CRF, anaesthetised by a 2nd year SHO in the middle of the night and sent back to the ward
86	TURP	Three previous MIs, hypertension on atenolol. SHO anaesthetist of more than two years' experience
39	Ileal conduit	Renal impairment, creatinine 189 μmol/L
76	TURBT	Hepatic metastases and renal impairment. Developed haematemesis and melaena postoperatively
75	Balloon dilatation of ureter through ileal conduit	IHD, CCF, and CRF (creatinine 308 μmol/L). GA. Hypotensive intra-operatively, given ephedrine and 2,500 ml of fluid over 90 minutes

Age

Age is not a specific contraindication to the use of NSAIDs. Many of the risks associated with NSAIDs do increase with age, for example GI bleeding and the risk of concurrent renal impairment, hypertension or cardiac failure. In this group of patients, the youngest patient prescribed NSAIDs was 36 and the oldest was 92 years. The proportion prescribed NSAIDs did not change with the patient's age until they were over 90 years.

Age	Total number	NSAIDs	Percentage
<60	183	24	*13.1*
60-69	241	35	*14.5*
70-79	474	66	*13.9*
80-89	338	51	*15.1*
>90	33	2	*6.1*

Renal impairment and known renal pathology

To quote from the Royal College of Anaesthetists (RCA) guidelines[50] (p. 10) "…it is clear that in the great majority of cases, use of NSAIDs for postoperative pain control will not jeopardise renal function. However, practising nephrologists recognise that a high proportion of cases of postoperative renal failure are associated with the use of NSAIDs. Rather than being the primary cause they are usually a contributory factor to the development of ARF *(acute renal failure)*." The guidelines list situations in which NSAIDs should be avoided, including renal impairment, hypovolaemia and circulatory failure. They also recommend caution in the use of NSAIDs in patients receiving ACE inhibitors, potassium-sparing diuretics and β-adrenergic blocking drugs. Renal function should be checked whenever renal impairment might be suspected.

Hypertension and cardiac failure

The RCA guidelines recommend that patients receiving treatment for hypertension or cardiac failure should be monitored closely if they are prescribed NSAIDs because NSAIDs cause fluid and water retention. In addition, concomitant diuretic administration increases the risk of renal toxicity.

GI ulceration and bleeding

GI problems are usually associated with long term use. However, GI bleeding or perforation should be a prominent differential diagnosis in all patients receiving NSAIDs. They should not be administered to patients with a history of GI ulceration or bleeding.

Haematological effects

NSAIDs increase bleeding time. The precise clinical significance of this is not clear.

Asthma

NSAIDs should not be used in patients with aspirin-sensitive asthma. They should be used with caution in other asthmatics.

It is impossible to assert that a patient would have recovered if NSAIDs had not been prescribed but clinicians must respect the contra-indications to the use of NSAIDs. The risks of renal impairment especially seem to be ignored. This needs to be appreciated by anaesthetists and surgeons. Some patients with raised creatinine levels were receiving diclofenac preoperatively on the ward. Other patients were prudently not prescribed NSAIDs by the anaesthetist, only for them to be prescribed by surgical ward staff postoperatively. Sick patients, especially if they are elderly, need immaculate care if they are to survive surgery.

Trainee anaesthetists supervising sedation for sick patients

> **Key message**
>
> - When deciding on the appropriate grade of anaesthetist the patient's condition should always be considered, together with the type of procedure and anaesthetic proposed.

Written by Dr Anthony Gray FRCA

Some patients requiring operation were correctly assessed as being very sick. It was assumed that general anaesthesia would impose great risks so their operation was carried out under local anaesthesia. In some of these, a junior anaesthetist was asked to provide sedation.

A 92-year-old man required decompression of a sigmoid volvulus. He had had a previous CVA. His current medical problems included an acute confusional state, atrial fibrillation, hypovolaemia, pre-renal renal failure, and a white blood count of $31.8\ x10^9.L^{-1}$. He was classed as ASA 4. A first year specialist registrar did not discuss the case with anyone. He gave *"analgesia and oxygen only"*. The patient died after 12 days from continuing pseudo-obstruction.

An 81-year-old man required open reduction and fixation of a fractured mandible. He had had a previous CVA, and suffered from ischaemic heart disease, congestive cardiac failure, diabetes, and chronic renal failure. Investigations showed a white count of $20.9\ x10^9.L^{-1}$, a serum sodium of $126\ mmol.L^{-1}$, serum glucose of $21.5\ mmol.L^{-1}$ and a creatinine of $209\ micromol.L^{-1}$. He was reported to be hypoxic on air, and was classed as *"ASA 3-4"*. A first year SHO did not discuss the case with anyone, although he wrote on the chart that it was *"an anaesthetic nightmare"*. He gave midazolam and ketamine whilst the operation was done under local anaesthesia. The patient died two days later.

A 76-year-old patient was scheduled for brachial embolectomy. He had a history of chronic obstructive pulmonary disease, congestive cardiac failure, and non-insulin dependent diabetes. His serum glucose was $23\ mmol.L^{-1}$, and his oxygen saturation was 85% despite oxygen being administered by a face mask. After discussion with a consultant, a second year SHO gave the patient 1 mg of midazolam during the operation, which finished at 13.00 hrs. In the recovery ward, the patient was unresponsive and noted to be *"dusky"*. He was returned to the ward. He died three hours later.

A 75-year-old patient with rheumatoid arthritis, chronic obstructive pulmonary disease and congestive cardiac failure developed rectal bleeding and required an oesophago-gastroscopy. She was attended by an SHO who had started training in anaesthesia five years before. He did not discuss the case with anybody. The patient was given 1 mg of midazolam and 40 mg of propofol. She died the next day.

A 54-year-old man had an inoperable rectal cancer with obstructive renal failure and a creatinine of $899\ micromol.L^{-1}$. His INR was 2.2. A first-year SHO attended whilst a ureteric stent was inserted. He discussed the case with the second on call. He gave the patient alfentanil, midazolam and pethidine. The man died 19 days after the operation.

An 84-year-old woman with chronic obstructive pulmonary disease, ischaemic heart disease and atrial fibrillation, assessed as ASA 4, required gastroscopy. No results of investigations were available. A second year SHO did not discuss the case with anyone. He sedated the woman with alfentanil 300 mcg and midazolam 1 mg and administered oxygen. She died the next day.

All of these patients were very ill and the anaesthetists were of limited experience. In some cases it is not clear what benefit the patient was expected to derive from the operation. In only two out of the six cases above did the trainee discuss the patient with a more senior colleague. Presumably an anaesthetist was asked to attend during the procedures because of the patients' poor general condition, the high probability that the patient would become over-sedated and unconscious, and the risk that a local anaesthetic might not be effective. However, in all of these cases it would have been quite inappropriate for the patients to have received a general anaesthetic from anaesthetists of such limited experience, so the anaesthetist present would be precisely the wrong person to deal with this complication. In addition, the anaesthetists were unaccompanied and so unable to obtain any educational benefit from the encounter.

As in all other areas of anaesthetic practice, if the surgical team request assistance, the decision as to the experience of anaesthetist required should be based on the patient's condition and not on the type of anaesthetic suggested by the surgeon.

Pathology

Advisors

Dr P N Cooper   (Newcastle upon Tyne)
Dr C M Corbishley   (London)
Dr N Francis   (London)
Dr J D Hemming   (Hexham)
Dr S Rogers   (Doncaster)
Dr R D Start   (Chesterfield)

Key messages

- The overall postmortem rate of 28% was very low.
- The hospital postmortem rate of 8% was unacceptably low.
- A small proportion of postmortem reports still did not include a clinicopathological correlation which should be present in all cases.
- Eighty-seven percent of postmortem reports were graded by the advisors as satisfactory or better.
- Histology is frequently not necessary particularly in Coroner's postmortem examinations.
- There is a need for a set of guidelines and some standardisation in formulating an OPCS cause of death in postoperative death cases.
- Variation in Coronial practice makes it impossible to build a single logical framework for deciding whether a case should be referred to HM Coroner.

Review process and sample

The members of the advisory group of consultant pathologists met on five occasions and reviewed a total of 301 postmortems of which 237 were performed for Her Majesty's Coroners and 64 for hospital doctors with the consent of the relatives of the deceased. A total of 474 cases out of the overall total of 1697 appeared from the surgical questionnaire to have had a postmortem performed so only 63% (301/474) of postmortem reports had been submitted for review. The overall postmortem rate was 28%.

The diverse nature of the six groups of cases reviewed this year makes any examination of the combined figures somewhat artificial. The value of comparison with previous years where different case types were selected is questionable. It would be useful to look at the same groups again in say 10 years time to see if there have been any changes or improvements. The groups will be referred to individually when appropriate.

Deaths reportable to the coroner and postmortem examination requests

The question numbers refer to those in the surgical questionnaire (see Appendix G).

Table PM1, question 50
Was the death reported to the Coroner?

Yes	742	*44%*
No	824	*49%*
Not answered	131	
Total	**1697**	

Deaths reported to the Coroner/specialty group

	Yes	No	Not answered	Total
Gynaecology	91	96	18	205
Head and neck surgery	126	143	46	315
Minimally invasive surgery	114	175	21	310
Oesophageal surgery	132	134	7	273
Spinal surgery	49	19	8	76
Urology	230	257	31	518
Total	**742**	**824**	**131**	**1697**

Table PM2, question 50a
If yes, was a Coroner's postmortem ordered and performed?

Yes	371	*50%*
No	343	*46%*
Not answered	28	
Total	**742**	

Forty-four percent of deaths were reported to the Coroner, a lower figure than in previous years.[48,51-53] The minimally invasive surgery group in particular had a very low referral rate, whereas the spinal surgery group had a high referral rate. Higher referral rates in previous years probably reflect different sample criteria. For example, all the cases in 1994/95, where the referral rate was 82%, were of deaths within three days of surgery.[53] Doctors are poor at recognising cases which should be referred to H.M. Coroner.[54] This is partly as a result of a lack of medicolegal education in the undergraduate curriculum.[55] A potentially even larger problem is the enormous variation in individual Coronial practice which means that it is not possible for a doctor moving from one Coroner's area to another over his career to build up a single logical decision-making framework when it comes to referral of a postoperative death to HM Coroner.

Referral would be greatly aided by a nationally agreed set of guidelines, probably by the centralisation of death-related matters within hospitals and possibly a routine review of individual deaths by a consultant pathologist.[56]

The percentage of cases referred which were accepted by the Coroner and a postmortem examination ordered (50%) is similar to that in previous years but did vary a little according to surgery type.

Table PM3, question 51
If a Coroner's postmortem examination was not performed, was a hospital postmortem examination undertaken?

Yes	103	8%
No	961	72%
Not answered	262	
Total	**1326**	

If no, why not? *(answers may be multiple)*

Cause of death/diagnosis known/no indication	434	45%
Relative-related	198	21%
"Not requested"/patient died under care of another doctor or at home	97	10%
Coroner felt not necessary	17	2%
Other	15	2%
Not stated	209	22%
Not known/not recorded	32	3%

Of those cases where a Coroner's postmortem was not performed only 8% had a hospital consent examination. This is similar to previous years remaining very low. Certainty as to the clinical diagnosis was again given as the commonest justification for not obtaining a postmortem despite a known high rate of discrepancies between such diagnoses and the results of postmortem examination. One would have hoped that, particularly in a relatively new area such as minimally invasive surgery, the clinicians would be more than usually interested in asking the relatives for permission for a postmortem examination. Factors likely to improve the hospital postmortem rate such as centralisation of death certification and regular clinicopathological meetings and a positive attitude to postmortem examinations by clinicians have previously been identified.[57] One reason for the low postmortem rate may be the fear of litigation based upon the findings. However, the availability of postmortem findings has on the contrary been shown to reduce both the number of claims and the cost of settlement where liability existed.[58,59]

Review of postmortem examination reports

The pathology advisory group again used the "Guidelines for Postmortem Reports" published by the Royal College of Pathologists in 1993[60] as the gold standard. The one exception to this was that some reports were still graded as excellent or very good in the absence of any histology. The guidelines recommend that histology should be performed on every postmortem but in some of the cases reviewed histology appeared unnecessary to the advisory group.

Clinical history

Table PM4
Is a clinical history provided?

	Coroner's		Hospital		Total	
Yes	202	85%	62	97%	264	88%
No	35	15%	2	3%	37	12%
Total	**237**		**64**		**301**	

When present, the clinical history is:

Unacceptably brief, obscure, uninformative	10	4%
Poor	24	9%
Satisfactory	68	26%
Good	60	23%
Fully detailed, clear, informative	102	38%
Total	**264**	

Once again, all cases were typewritten. A clinical history was provided in all but two of the hospital postmortem examinations but was absent in 15% of the Coroner's postmortem examinations. This must in part reflect the fact that some Coroners forbid or discourage their pathologists from including a clinical history and there is perhaps increasing concern amongst pathologists that they might be said to be overstepping their remit by interpreting clinical evidence.[61] When present, the clinical history was satisfactory or better in 87% of cases.

External examination

Table PM5
The description of external appearance is:

Unacceptably brief, inadequately detailed	15	*5%*
Poor	41	*14%*
Satisfactory	95	*31%*
Good	78	*26%*
Fully detailed, clear, informative	72	*24%*
Total	**301**	

Table PM6
Were scars and incisions measured?

Yes	172	*57%*
No	69	*23%*
Not applicable	60	*20%*
Total	**301**	

The external examination was described as poor or inadequate in almost one fifth of cases (similar figures for both Coroner's and hospital postmortem examinations). Scars and incisions were measured in over two thirds of the cases where relevant. There was disagreement amongst the advisory group as to whether it was necessary to measure scars.

Internal examination

Table PM7
The gross description of internal organs is:

Unacceptably brief, inadequately detailed	8	*2%*
Poor	35	*12%*
Satisfactory	87	*29%*
Good	96	*32%*
Fully detailed, clear, informative	75	*25%*
Total	**301**	

The description of internal organs was satisfactory or better in 85% of cases, similar to previous years.

Table PM8
Number of organs weighed (paired organs count as 1)

None	21	7%
1	11	4%
2	14	5%
3	14	5%
4	19	6%
5	43	14%
6	141	47%
7	17	5%
8	14	5%
9	6	2%
more than 9	1	<1%
Total	**301**	

Table PM9

Were the skull and brain examined?

	Coroner's		Hospital		Total	
Yes	218	92%	54	84%	272	90%
No	17	7%	10	16%	27	9%
Not known	2				2	
Total	**237**		**64**		**301**	

Sixteen percent of hospital postmortem examinations did not include examination of the skull and brain, at least some of which were cases where permission specifically excluded this examination. The 7% of Coroner's postmortem examinations where the skull and brain were not examined is identical to that from 1994/95.[53]

Table PM10
Is the operation site described?

Yes	237	79%
No	44	15%
Full notes not available	20	
Total	**301**	

The operation site was not described in 15% of cases. A postmortem examination report should always include this information but in some of the cases this year it may have been missed out simply because of the relatively minor nature of the surgery (endoscopy, tracheostomy, TURP).

Table PM11
Is the gross examination appropriate to the clinical problem?

Yes	289	96%
No	10	3%
Full notes not available	2	
Total	**301**	

Additional investigations

Table PM12 *(answers may be multiple)*
Samples were taken for:

	Coroner's		Hospital		Total	
Histology	72	30%	31	48%	103	34%
Microbiology	4		3		7	2%
Toxicology	4		-		4	1%
None of these investigations	162		33		195	65%
Total	**237**		**64**		**301**	

Table PM13 *(answers may be multiple)*
A thorough postmortem examination in this case would have called for:

	Coroner's			Hospital			Total		
	Called for	Sample taken		Called for	Sample taken		Called for	Sample taken	
Histology	234	71	30%	62	29	47%	296	100	34
Microbiology	7	3		9	3		16	6	
Toxicology	2	2		-	-		2	2	
Total	**237**			**64**			**301**		

Table PM14
Is a histological report included with the postmortem examination report?

	Coroner's		Hospital		Total	
Yes	49	21%	24	31%	73	24%
No	188	79%	40	69%	228	76%
Total	**237**		**64**		**301**	

When present, the histological report is:

Unacceptably brief, inadequately detailed	-	
Poor	3	4%
Satisfactory	24	33%
Good	13	18%
Fully detailed, clear, informative	33	45%
Total	**73**	

When absent, does the lack of histology detract significantly from the value of this report?

	Coroner's		Hospital		Total	
Yes	28	15%	16	40%	44	19%
No	160	85%	24	60%	184	81%
Total	**188**		**40**		**228**	

Samples were taken for histology in 48% of hospital cases and 30% of Coroner's cases, higher figures than in preceding years but a histology report was included with the postmortem report in a much smaller proportion of cases. There was often evidence that histology had been taken and in many cases additional histology reports were probably issued but not sent to NCEPOD. The figures in Table PM13 assume that histology should have been done in all cases as suggested by the College guidelines but the figures in Table PM14 show that in Coroners' postmortem examinations, in the opinion of the advisors, the absence of histology was probably not important in 85% of cases. In 40% of hospital cases where it had not been performed it was thought that it would have been useful. There were many cases where surgical specimens had been removed in life and therefore some histological evidence had been gathered. There is considerable discrepancy here between the value of histology as seen by the pathology advisory group and that recommended by the Royal College of Pathologists. Whatever the postmortem examination type, histology has to be cost effective.[62]

The postmortem report

1. SUMMARY

Table PM15
Is a summary of the lesions present?

Yes	100	*33%*
No	201	*67%*
Total	**301**	

When present, does this correspond accurately to the text report?

Yes	95	*95%*
No	2	*2%*
Full notes not available	3	
Total	**100**	

A separate summary of lesions was only present in 33% of cases but in some cases a form of summary was included within the text of the clinicopathological correlation. The percentage where a summary was present was considerably higher than the preceding year. The College guidelines recommend that such a summary is always present. Perhaps the guidelines are having an effect.

2. THE CAUSE OF DEATH

Table PM16
Is an OPCS cause of death present?

Yes	283	*94%*
No	18	*6%*
Total	**301**	

When present, does it correspond accurately to the text report?

	Coroner's		Hospital		Total	
Yes	218	*92%*	45	*96%*	**263**	*93%*
No	14	*6%*	2	*4%*	**16**	*6%*
Not clear	4		-		**4**	
Total	**236**		**47**		**283**	

Does it follow OPCS formatting rules?

	Coroner's		Hospital		Total	
Yes	227	*96%*	46	*98%*	**273**	*96%*
No	9	*4%*	1	*2%*	**10**	*4%*
Total	**236**		**47**		**283**	

An OPCS format cause of death was present in 94% of cases. Seventeen of the 18 cases where it was absent were hospital postmortem examinations, some of which were only partial examinations. The guidelines for postmortem examination reports state that it is good practice to include an OPCS cause of death. In many hospital postmortem examinations the death certificate is completed prior to the examination and sometimes the pathologist may feel it inappropriate to formulate a cause of death particularly if the examination is limited.

The cause of death when present was regarded as well formulated and accurate. However, it was apparent that there was widespread variation in practice between pathologists, including the advisors, particularly with respect to where and whether the operative procedure was mentioned in the cause of death. There was frequent use of the formula whereby the disease for which the operation was performed was given as the cause of death with "operated on" … in brackets after the disease. This variation presumably reflected local practice, particularly the preference of the Coroner.

Formulating the cause of death can be difficult. There is the additional pressure on the pathologist of knowing that often the manner in which the cause of death is formulated decides whether there will be an inquest. Postoperative deaths are frequently complicated but the pathologist's position is particularly difficult if he has inadequate clinical information, has to interpret complex clinical events or has not had the opportunity of discussing the case with the surgeon. It has been argued that where the cause of death requires interpretation of the clinical history, a pathologist should refrain from giving a cause of death; such a task is for the court.[61] It is certainly not the responsibility of the pathologist to decide whether an inquest is necessary.

Depending on local Coronial practice when formulating a cause of death the pathologist may need to take into account whether the surgery was emergency or elective, whether an error occurred, whether the fatal complication is regarded as "recognised" and whether there are allegations of negligence. These matters provoked lively discussion amongst the members of the group with little agreement. One basic problem is the lack of a consistent, clear purpose within the Coroners' system[63] perhaps particularly in relation to the investigation of postoperative deaths.

3.   CLINICOPATHOLOGICAL CORRELATION

Table PM17
Is a clinicopathological correlation present?

Yes	197	*65%*
No	104	*35%*
Total	**301**	

If yes, the clinicopathological correlation is:

Unacceptably brief, obscure, uninformative	3	*1%*
Poor	9	*5%*
Satisfactory	63	*32%*
Good	57	*29%*
Fully detailed, clear, informative	65	*33%*
Total	**197**	

A clinicopathological correlation was present in a higher percentage of cases than previously (65%) but absent in 34% of hospital cases surprisingly considering that in many cases it is the only part of the report read by the clinician. In a postoperative death every postmortem examination report should contain a clinicopathological correlation, even if only a sentence or two, indicating whether the procedure played any part in the death and whether anything untoward or unexpected had happened. When present the correlation was felt to be satisfactory or better in virtually all cases and in one third was described as fully detailed, clear and informative, a much higher percentage than previous years.

Table PM18
Overall score for the postmortem examinations

	Total	
Unacceptable, laying the pathologist open to serious professional criticism	7	*2%*
Poor	34	*11%*
Satisfactory	108	*36%*
Good	112	*37%*
Excellent, meeting all standards set by RCPath guidelines	40	*13%*
Total	**301**	

Table PM19
Overall score for the postmortem examinations by grade of pathologist (from SQ)

	Overall Score									Total
	Unsatisfactory		Poor		Satisfactory		Good		Excellent	
Consultant	7	*3%*	30	*11%*	98	*36%*	102	*37%*	36	*13%*	273
Junior	-	*0%*	-	*0%*	7	*50%*	5	*36%*	2	*14%*	14
Not answered	-		3		-		3		2		
Not known / not recorded	-		1		3		2		-		
Total	**7**		**34**		**108**		**112**		**40**		**301**

Eighty-seven percent of postmortem examinations were graded as satisfactory or better with the only difference to previous years being that in our figures 13% were graded as excellent, a much higher proportion than before probably reflecting our slightly "looser" interpretation of the need for histology. Seven postmortem examinations, all Coroners', were graded as unacceptable and laid the pathologist open to serious professional criticism. Several cases could not be assessed properly because of the restraints placed upon the pathologist's report by the Coroner, i.e. he only allowed a cause of death to be issued. All the small number of postmortem examinations performed by trainee pathologists were satisfactory or better.

Table PM20 *(answers may be multiple)*
When the history, antemortem clinical diagnosis and cause of death are compared with the postmortem findings, this postmortem demonstrates:

	Coroner's		Hospital		Total	
A discrepancy in the cause of death or in a major diagnosis, which if known, might have affected treatment, outcome or prognosis	14	*6%*	3	*5%*	**17**	*6%*
A discrepancy in the cause of death or in a major diagnosis, which if known, would probably **not** have affected treatment, outcome or prognosis	33	*14%*	8	*13%*	**41**	*14%*
A minor discrepancy	4	*2%*	-	*0%*	**4**	*1%*
Confirmation of essential clinical findings	175	*74%*	52	*81%*	**227**	*75%*
An interesting incidental finding	11	*5%*	7	*11%*	**18**	*6%*
A failure to explain some important aspect of the clinical problem, as a result of a **satisfactory** postmortem	4	*2%*	3	*5%*	**7**	*2%*
A failure to explain some important aspect of the clinical problem, as a result of an **unsatisfactory** postmortem	10	*4%*	-	*0%*	**10**	*3%*
Other	1		-		-	

A small percentage of postmortem examinations showed a discrepancy which if known might have affected treatment, outcome or prognosis with a very large percentage confirming the principal clinical findings. These figures are very similar to previous years. The totally unexpected postmortem examination findings included leakage of TPN fluid into the pericardial sac; an unsuspected acute myocardial infarct; a jejunostomy leaking into the peritoneal cavity; an unexpected dilated cardiomyopathy; peritonitis due to traumatic perforation of the ileum; septicaemia due to an unsuspected perforated duodenal ulcer; unsuspected peritonitis from a gastrostomy tube; acute gastric dilatation; unsuspected pneumonia and peritonitis due to small bowel perforation. Many of these were in relatively minor procedures such as gastrostomy, illustrating the importance of leaving tubes and lines in situ prior to the postmortem examination.

Transmission of the postmortem examinations findings

Table PM21, question 52
Was the surgical team informed of the date and time of the postmortem?

	Coroners' postmortems		Hospital postmortems		All postmortems	
Yes	123	_33%_	50	_49%_	173	_36%_
No	221		44		265	
Not answered	27		9		36	
Total	**371**		**103**		**474**	

Table PM22, question 52a _(answers may be multiple)_
If yes, which member of the surgical team attended the postmortem?

None	75	_43%_
House officer	12	_7%_
Senior house officer	22	_13%_
Specialist registrar	25	_14%_
Staff grade	1	_1%_
Clinical assistant	2	_1%_
Associate specialist	4	_2%_
Consultant	33	_19%_
Other	6	_3%_
Not answered	7	_4%_
Total	**173**	

Table PM23, question 53 _(answers may be multiple)_
If a surgeon did not attend the postmortem, why not?
(Only for those cases where the surgical team was informed of the date and time of the postmortem but none of the surgical team attended)

Unavailable/other commitments	45	_60%_
Nothing to be gained/diagnosis known	10	_13%_
Other	13	_17%_
Not answered	4	
Not known/not recorded	3	
Total	**75**	

Table PM24, question 54
Did the surgical team receive a copy of the postmortem report?

Yes	360	76%
Informal report/verbal message	33	7%
No	73	
Not answered	8	
Total	**474**	

In only a third of cases was the surgical team informed of the date and time of the postmortem. This was a figure similar to preceding years with Coroners' postmortems less well communicated. This low percentage did raise the issue of cases where the postmortem is done other than at the hospital where the operation was performed. This is, in terms of clinicopathological continuity, an undesirable occurrence. In several cases in the surgical questionnaire the surgeon stated that he had either been forbidden from attending the postmortem or felt that his presence was not allowed as he might influence the pathologist's judgement. In fact the Coroners' Rules (1984)[64] list the "deceased's' regular medical attendant" and "the hospital" (if the death occurred in hospital) amongst those to be notified by the Coroner when a postmortem is to be performed. These individuals/institutions have the right to be represented at the postmortem by a medical practitioner or in the case of a doctor to attend themselves.[64]

In a quarter of cases the surgical team did not receive a copy of the postmortem report. This figure was very similar for hospital and Coroners' postmortems. There is no obvious explanation for this in the case of hospital postmortems but the attitude of Coroners to the dissemination of postmortem findings does vary. Some will not allow a report to be released. Others only after an inquest has been held. In some cases the surgeon filling in the surgical questionnaire may not have known that a report had been received by another member of the clinical team.

Table PM25, question 54a/question 44
How long after the patient's death was the first information received, giving the results of the postmortem?

	Coroner's postmortems		Hospital postmortems		All postmortems	
7 days or less	90	24%	28	27%	**118**	25%
8 days to 30 days	43	12%	23	22%	**66**	14%
31 days to 60 days	15	4%	3	3%	**18**	4%
More than 60 days	28	8%	6	6%	**34**	7%
Not answered*	195	53%	43	42%	**238**	50%
Total	**371**		**103**		**474**	

* may indicate that no written information was received

The College guidelines recommend that initial information is transmitted to the clinician within a maximum of two days.

Table PM26, Question 56

Did the pathological information confirm the clinical impression?

	Coroner's postmortems		Hospital postmortems		All postmortems	
Yes	271	*73%*	75	*73%*	**346**	*73%*
No	60	*16%*	14	*14%*	**74**	*16%*
Not known/not recorded	26		8		**34**	
Not answered*	14		6		**20**	
Total	**371**		**103**		**474**	

* *may indicate that no written information was received*

In three-quarters of cases the postmortem examinations confirmed the clinical findings but in 16% of cases there were significant unexpected findings.

References

1 Hall V, Overton C, Hargreaves J, Maresh MJA *Hysterectomy in the treatment of dysfunctional uterine bleeding.* British Journal of Obstetrics & Gynaecology 1998 (vol 105) supp 17; page 16

2 *Report of the RCOG Working Party on prophylaxis against thromboembolism in gynaecology and obstetrics.* Ed: RW Shaw. London, 1995.

3 *Low molecular weight heparins for venous thromboembolism.* Drugs Therapeutics Bulletin. 1998;**36**:25-29.

4 Standing Medical Advisory Committee: *Report on the management of ovarian cancer, current clinical practices.* 1991.

5 *Report of the joint working party on anaesthesia in ophthalmic surgery.* Royal College of Anaesthetists & College of Ophthalmologists. London 1993.

6 Benumof JL. *Laryngeal mask airway and the ASA difficult airway algorithm.* Anesthesiology 1996; **84**:686-699

7 Data provided to NCEPOD by Hospital Episode Statistics (Department of Health).

8 Freeland AP, Bates GJ. *The surgical treatment of a pharyngeal pouch: inversion or excision?* Annals RCS Eng 1987; 69:57-58.

9 Koay CB, Bates GJ. *Endoscopic stapling diverticulotomy for pharyngeal pouch.* Clin Otolaryngol. 1996;**21**:371-6.

10 Baldwin DD, Toma AG. *Endoscopic stapled diverticulotomy: a real advance in the treatment of hypopharyngeal diverticulum.* Clin Otolaryngol 1998;**23**:244-47.

11 North American Symptomatic Carotid Endarterectomy Trial Collaborators. *Beneficial effect of carotid endarterectomy in symptomatic patients with high grade stenosis.* N Engl J Med 1991;**325**:445-53.

12 European Carotid Surgery Trialists' Collaborative Group. *Randomised trial of endarterectomy for recently symptomatic carotid stenosis: final results of the MRC European Carotid Surgery Trial (ECST).* Lancet 1998;**351**:1379-87

13 Royal College of Surgeons of England. *Guidelines for clinicians on medical records and notes.* London: RCS Eng, 1994.

14 Tangkanakul C, Counsell C, Warlow C. *Carotid endarterectomy performed under local anaesthetic compared to general anaesthetic (Cochrane Review).* In: The Cochrane Library, Issue 3, 1998. Oxford: Update Software.

15 Kaw M, Sekas G. *Long-term follow-up of consequences of percutaneous endoscopic gastrostomy (PEG) tubes in nursing home patients.* Dig Dis Sci 1994;**39**:738-43.

16 Light VL, Slezak FA, Porter JA, Gerson LW. *Predictive factors for early mortality after percutaneous endoscopic gastrostomy.* Gastrointest Endosc 1995;**42**:330-5.

17 Bourdel-Marchasson I, Dumas F, Pinganaud G, Emeriau JP, Decamps A. *Audit of percutaneous endoscopic gastrostomy in long-term enteral feeding in a nursing home.* Int J Qual Health Care 1997;**9**:297-302.

18   Rabeneck L, Wray NP, Petersen NJ. *Long-term outcomes of patients receiving percutaneous endoscopic gastrostomy tubes.* J Gen Intern Med 1996;**11**:287-93.

19   Jarnagin WR, Duh QY, Mulvihill SJ, Ridge JA, Schrock TR, Way LW. *The efficacy and limitations of percutaneous endoscopic gastrostomy.* Arch Surg 1992;**127**:261-4.

20   Fay DE, Poplausky M, Gruber M, Lance P. *Long-term enteral feeding: a retrospective comparison of delivery via percutaneous endoscopic gastrostomy and nasoenteric tubes.* Am J Gastroenterol 1991;**86**:1604-9.

21   Nair RG, Dunn DC, Fowler S, McCloy RF. *Progress with cholecystectomy: improving results in England and Wales.* Br J Surg 1997;**84**:1396-8

22   Wahba RW, Beique F, Kleiman SJ. *Cardiopulmonary function and laparoscopic cholecystectomy.* Can J Anaes 1995;**42**:51-63.

23   Begos DG, Franco KL, Baldwin JC, Lee FA, Revkin JH, Modlin IM. *Optimal timing and indications for cholecystectomy in cardiac transplant patients.* World J Surg 1995;**19**:661-7.

24   Dexter SPL, Martin IG, Marton J, McMahon MJ. *Long operation and the risks from laparoscopic cholecystectomy.* Br J Surg 1997;**84**:464-6.

25   Williamson WA et al. *Barrett's oesophagus. Prevalence and incidence of adenocarcinoma.* Arch Int Med 1991;**151**:2212-6

26   Streitz JM, Andrews CW, Ellis FHJ. *Endoscopic surveillance of Barrett's oesophagus. Does it help?* Journal of Thoracic and Cardiovascular Surgery 1993;**105**:383.

27   Hoff SJ et al. *Prognosis of adenocarcinoma arising in Barrett's oesophagus.* Annals of Thoracic Surgery 1998;**65**:176-9.

28   Merger RS, Merger D. *Carcinoma of the oesophagus and tylosis. A lethal genetic combination.* Cancer 1993; **72**:17.

29   Streitz JM, Ellis FH, Gibb PS, Heatley GM. *Achalasia and squamous cell carcinoma of the oesophagus. Analysis of 241 patients.* Annals of Thoracic Surgery, 1995;**59**:1604-9.

30   Choi TK, Siu KF, Lam KH. *Bronchoscopy and carcinoma of the oesophagus.* American Journal of Surgery 1984;**147**:757.

31   Dittler HJ, Stewart JR. *Role of endoscopic ultrasonography in oesophageal cancer.* Endoscopy 1993;**25**:156.

32   Muller JM, Erasmitt, Steizner M, Zieren U, Pichlmaier H. *Surgical therapy of oesophageal cancer.* Br J Surg 1990; 77: 845-857.

33   O'Hanlon DM, Karat D, Shaw I, Scott D, Griffin SM. *Oesophagectomy: results from a single UK centre.* Br J Surg 1997; 84 (supplement 1): 14.

34   Harrington KD. (1981). *The use of methylmethacrylate for vertebral body replacement and anterior stabilisation of pathologic fracture dislocation of the spine due to malignant disease.* J Bone Joint Surgery 63A: 36-47.

35   Kostwick JP. (1983). *Anterior spinal cord compression for lesions of the thoracic and lumbar spine.* Spine 8: 512-531.

36   Barron KD, Hirano A, Avaki S, Terry RD, (1989). *Experience with metastatic neoplasms involving the spinal cord.* Neurology 9: 91-106.

37   Constans JP, DeDivitiis E, Dozelli R, Spaziante R, Mider JF, Hayer C. (1983). *Spinal metastasis with neurological manifestations. Review of 600 cases.* J Neurosurg 59: 11-118.

38   DeWald RL, Bridwell KM, Prodromas C, Rodts MF (1985). *Reconstruction spinal surgery as palliation for metastatic malignancies of the spine.* Spine 10: 21-26.

39   Fidler MW, (1986). *Anterior decompression and stabilisation of metastatic spinal fractures.* J Bone Joint Surgery 68B: 83-90.

40   Siegal T, Tigra P, Siegal T. (1985). *Vertebral body resection for epidural compression by malignant tumours.* J bone Joint Surg 67A: 375-382.

41   Tomita K, Toribatake Y, Kawanava N, Ohnari H, Kobe H. (1994). *Total en block spondylectomy and circum spinal decompression for solitary spinal metastasis.* Paraplegia 31: 36-46.

42   Turner PL, Prince HG, Webb JK, Sokal MPJW. (1988). *Surgery for malignant extradural tumours of the spine.* J Bone Joint Surg 70B: 451-456.

43   Enkaova E A, Doursounian L, Chatellier G, Mabesoone F, Aimard T, Saillent G. (1997) *A critical appreciation of the pre-operative prognostic Takuhashi Score in a series of 71 cases.* Spine 22: 2293-2298.

44   Hammerberg KW. (1992). *Surgical treatment of metastatic spine disease.* Spine 17: 1148-1153.

45   Takuhashi Y, Matsuzaki H, Toriyama S, Kawano H, Ohsaka S. (1990). *Scoring system for the pre-operative evaluation of metastatic spine tumour prognosis.* Spine 15: 1110-1113.

46   Kostwick JP, Errico JN, Gleason TF, Errico CC. (1988) *Spinal stabilisation of vertebral body tumours.* Spine 13: 250-256.

47   McLain R F, Wernstein JN. (1990). *Tumours of the spine.* Semin. Spine Surg 2: 157-180.

48   Campling EA, Devlin HB, Hoile RW, Lunn JN. *The Report of the National Confidential Enquiry into Perioperative Deaths 1991/1992.* London 1993.

49   *The Report of the National Confidential Enquiry into Perioperative Deaths 1993/1994.* NCEPOD. London, 1996.

50   The Royal College of Anaesthetists. *Guidelines for the Use of Non-steroidal Anti-inflammatory Drugs in the Perioperative Period.* The Royal College of Anaesthetists, London 1998

51   Campling EA, Devlin HB, Hoile RW, Lunn JN. *The Report of the National Confidential Enquiry into Perioperative Deaths 1992/1993.* London, 1995.

52   *The Report of the National Confidential Enquiry into Perioperative Deaths 1993/1994.* NCEPOD. London, 1996.

53   Gallimore SC, Hoile RW, Ingram GS, Sherry KM. *The Report of the National Confidential Enquiry into Perioperative Deaths 1994/1995.* London, 1997.

54   Start RD, Dalargy-Aziz Y, Dorries CP, *et al. Clinicians and the coronial system: ability of clinicians to recognise reportable deaths.* British Medical Journal 1993; **306:** 1038-1041.

55   Knight B, Thompson IM. *The teaching of legal medicine in British medical schools*. Medical Education 1986; **20:** 246-258.

56   Leadbeatter S, Knight B. *Reporting deaths to Coroners: all the legal aspects of dying need re-examining*. British Medical Journal 1993; **306:** 1018.

57   Champ C, Tyler X, Andrews PS, Coghill SB. *Improve your hospital postmortem rate to 40-50 per cent, a tale of two towns*. Journal of Pathology 1992; **166:** 405-407.

58   Lord JT. *Risk management in pathology and laboratory medicine*. Arch Pathol Lab Med 1990; **114:** 1164-1167.

59   Valaske MJ. Loss control/risk management: a survey of the contribution of postmortem examination. *Arch Pathol Lab Med* 1984; **108:** 462-468.

60   The Royal College of Pathologists. *Guidelines for Postmortem Reports*. London, The Royal College of Pathologists, 1993.

61   James DS, Leadbeatter S. *The use of personal health information in the Coroner's inquiry*. Journal of the Royal College of Physicians of London 1997; **31:** 509-511.

62   Reid WA. Cost effectiveness of routine postmortem histology. *Journal of Clinical Pathology* 1987; 40: 459-461.

63   Cordner SM, Loff B. 800 years of coroners: have they a future? *The Lancet* 1994; **344:** 799-801.

64   *The Coroners Rules 1984.*

Appendix A - Glossary

Definition of the 1996/97 sample groups

Gynaecology – any gynaecological procedure.

Head and neck surgery – any procedure in the head and neck region including the base of skull and pharyngeal pouch surgery but excluding intracranial operations.

Minimally invasive surgery – the sample for this group was difficult to define as much debate remains about the most accurate title for this form of surgery, which is variously called minimally invasive surgery, minimal access surgery, endoscopic surgery, laparoscopic surgery and keyhole surgery. We have included minimal access general abdominal surgery, endoscopic thoracic and orthopaedic surgery and diagnostic or therapeutic endoscopies (excluding gynaecological laparoscopy and urological endoscopy).

Oesophageal surgery – any oesophageal procedure including specific oesophageal endoscopy.

Spinal surgery – any spinal procedure.

Urology – any urological procedure including urological endoscopy.

Admission

Elective - at a time agreed between the patient and the surgical service.

Urgent - within 48 hours of referral/consultation.

Emergency - immediately following referral/consultation, when admission is unpredictable and at short notice because of clinical need.

American Society of Anesthesiologists (ASA) Classification of Physical Status

ASA 1 a normal healthy patient.

ASA 2 a patient with mild systemic disease.

ASA 3 a patient with severe systemic disease that limits activity but is not incapacitating.

ASA 4 a patient with incapacitating systemic disease that is a constant threat to life.

ASA 5 a moribund patient who is not expected to survive for 24 hours with or without an operation.

(NCEPOD) Classification of operations

Emergency

Immediate life-saving operation, resuscitation simultaneous with surgical treatment (e.g. trauma, ruptured aortic aneurysm). Operation usually within one hour.

Urgent

Operation as soon as possible after resuscitation (e.g. irreducible hernia, intussuception, oesophageal atresia, intestinal obstruction, major fractures). Operation within 24 hours.

Scheduled

An early operation but not immediately life-saving (e.g. malignancy). Operation usually within three weeks.

Elective

Operation at a time to suit both patient and surgeon (e.g. cholecystectomy, joint replacement).

Out of hours

NCEPOD's definition of out-of-hours operating includes all operations started between 18.01 and 07.59 on a weekday, as well as operations performed at any time on a Saturday or Sunday.

Recovery and special care areas

(Definitions used by the Association of Anaesthetists of Great Britain and Ireland)

High dependency unit

A high dependency unit (HDU) is an area for patients who require more intensive observation, treatment and nursing care than can be provided on a general ward. It would not normally accept patients requiring mechanical ventilation, but could manage those receiving invasive monitoring.

Intensive care unit

An intensive care unit (ICU) is an area to which patients are admitted for treatment of actual or impending organ failure, especially when mechanical ventilation is necessary.

Recovery area

A recovery area is an area to which patients are admitted from an operating theatre, and where they remain until consciousness has been regained, respiration and circulation are stable and postoperative analgesia is established.

Appendix B - Abbreviations

AAA	Abdominal aortic aneurysm
ACE (inhibitors)	Angiotensin-converting enzyme
AF	Atrial fibrillation
ASA	American Society of Anesthesiologists
BP	Blood pressure
BSO	Bilateral salpingo-oophorectomy
CABG	Coronary artery bypass graft
CCF	Congestive cardiac failure
CCU	Coronary care unit
COAD	Chronic obstructive airway disease
COPD	Chronic obstructive pulmonary disease
CPAP	Continuous positive airways pressure
CRF	Chronic renal failure
CT	Computerised tomography
CVA	Cerebro vascular accident
CVP	Central venous pressure
D & C	Dilatation and curettage
DU	Duodenal ulcer
DVT	Deep vein thrombosis
ECG	Electrocardiogram
ERCP	Endoscopic retrograde cholangio-pancreatography
EUA	Examination under anaesthesia
FEV1	Forced expiratory volume, one second
FNAC	Fine needle aspiration cytology
GA	General anaesthetic
GI	Gastrointestinal
GU	Genito-urinary
HDU	High dependency unit
ICU	Intensive care unit
IDDM	Insulin-dependent diabetes mellitus
IHD	Ischaemic heart disease
IM	Intramuscular
INR	International normalised ratio
LA	Local anaesthetic
LVF	Left ventricular failure

MI	Myocardial infarction
MRI	Magnetic resonance imaging
MRSA	Methicillin resistant staphylococcus aureus
MUA	Manipulation under anaesthesia
NIDDM	Non-insulin-dependent diabetes mellitus
NIRS	Near infra-red spectroscopy
NMR	Nuclear magnetic resonance imaging
NSAID	Non-steroidal anti-inflammatory drug
OCTT	Oral cuffed tracheal tube
OGD	Oesophago-gastro-duodenoscopy
OLV	One lung ventilation
ORIF	Open reduction and internal fixation
PA	Posterior anterior
PCA	Patient controlled analgesia
PE	Pulmonary embolism
PEEP	Positive end expiratory pressure
PEG	Percutaneous endoscopic gastrostomy
PM	Postmortem
POSSUM	Physiological and operative severity score for enumeration of mortality and morbidity
RTA	Road traffic accident
SAP	Systolic arterial pressure
SHO	Senior house officer
SOB	Short of breath
SpR 1,2,3,4	Specialist Registrar, years 1, 2, 3 and 4
TAH	Total abdominal hysterectomy
TCC	Transitional cell carcinoma
TCD	Trans-cranial Doppler
TIA	Transient ischaemic attack
TLV	Two lung ventilation
TPN	Total parenteral nutrition
TURBT	Transurethral resection of bladder tumour
TURP	Transurethral resection of prostate

Appendix C - NCEPOD Corporate structure

The National Confidential Enquiry into Perioperative Deaths (NCEPOD) is an independent body to which a corporate commitment has been made by the Associations, Colleges and Faculties related to its areas of activity. Each of these bodies nominates members of the Steering Group.

Steering Group (as at 1 October 1998)

Chairman
Emeritus Professor V R Tindall CBE

Other members

Mrs M Beck	(Royal College of Ophthalmologists)
Dr J F Dyet	(Royal College of Radiologists)
Dr M J Goldacre	(Faculty of Public Health Medicine)
Dr H H Gray	(Royal College of Physicians of London)
Mr G T Layer	(Association of Surgeons of Great Britain and Ireland)
Professor V J Lund	(Royal College of Surgeons of England)
Dr J M Millar	(Royal College of Anaesthetists)
Dr A J Mortimer	(Royal College of Anaesthetists)
Mr J H Shepherd	(Royal College of Obstetricians and Gynaecologists)
Dr P J Simpson	(Royal College of Anaesthetists)
Mr M F Sullivan	(Royal College of Surgeons of England)
Professor P G Toner	(Royal College of Pathologists)
Professor T Treasure	(Royal College of Surgeons of England)
Dr D J Wilkinson	(Association of Anaesthetists of Great Britain and Ireland)
Mr J Ll Williams	(Faculty of Dental Surgery, Royal College of Surgeons of England)

Observers

Dr P A Knapman	(Coroners' Society of England and Wales)
Dr V Chishty	(Department of Health - England)

NCEPOD is a company limited by guarantee, managed by the Trustees.

Trustees

Chairman	Professor V R Tindall
Treasurer	Dr J N Lunn
	Dr J Lumley
	Mr J Ll Williams

Clinical Coordinators

The Steering Group appoint the Principal Clinical Coordinators for a defined tenure. The Principal Clinical Coordinators lead the review of the data relating to the annual sample and advise the Steering Group and write the reports. They may also from time to time appoint Clinical Coordinators, who must be engaged in active academic/clinical practice (in the NHS) during the full term of office.

Principal Clinical Coordinators

Anaesthesia	Dr G S Ingram
Surgery	Mr R W Hoile

Clinical Coordinators

Anaesthesia	Dr A J G Gray
	Dr K M Sherry
Surgery	Mr K G Callum
	Mr I C Martin

Funding

The total annual cost of NCEPOD is approximately £450,000 (1997/98). We are pleased to acknowledge the continued support of;

Department of Health (England)
Welsh Office
Health and Social Services Executive (Northern Ireland)
States of Guernsey Board of Health
Jersey Group of Hospitals
Department of Health and Social Security, Isle of Man Government
BUPA Hospitals Limited
Benenden Hospital
Nuffield Hospitals
St Martins Hospitals Limited
The London Clinic

This funding covers the *total* cost of the Enquiry, including administrative salaries and reimbursements for clinical coordinators, office accommodation charges, computer and other equipment as well as travelling and other expenses for the coordinators, Steering Group and advisory groups.

Appendix D - Protocol

The National Confidential Enquiry into Perioperative Deaths

(Protocol revised July 1996)

The National Confidential Enquiry into Perioperative Deaths (NCEPOD) is an independent body, launched in 1988, to which a corporate commitment has been made by the Associations, Colleges and Faculties related to its areas of activity. NCEPOD was incorporated in February 1995 as a company limited by guarantee.

NCEPOD is independent of the Departments of Health and of the other governmental and non-governmental organizations which support it financially. The Enquiry reviews clinical practice across England, Wales, Northern Ireland, Jersey, Guernsey and the Isle of Man. All NHS and Defence Medical Services hospitals are included as well as those managed by BUPA Hospitals Ltd, General Healthcare Group PLC, Nuffield Hospitals, St Martins Ltd, Benenden Hospital and Wellington Hospital.

Management of the Enquiry

NCEPOD is overseen by a Steering Group, the members of which are nominated by the following Associations, Colleges and Faculties:

> Association of Anaesthetists of Great Britain and Ireland
> Association of Surgeons of Great Britain and Ireland
> Royal College of Anaesthetists
> Royal College of Obstetricians and Gynaecologists
> Royal College of Ophthalmologists
> Royal College of Physicians of London
> Royal College of Pathologists
> Royal College of Radiologists
> Royal College of Surgeons of England
> Faculty of Dental Surgery of the Royal College of Surgeons of England
> Faculty of Public Health Medicine of the Royal Colleges of Physicians of the UK

The Steering Group's responsibilities include agreement of the definition and method of the annual sample for detailed study and approval of the reports published by NCEPOD.

The Steering Group members appoint Trustees who are responsible for the management of the Enquiry and its business as specified in the Memorandum and Articles of Association.

Method of the Enquiry

The protocol, agreed in December 1988, was derived from that of the Confidential Enquiry into Perioperative Deaths (CEPOD), the report of which was published in December 1987.

The Enquiry reviews clinical practice and aims to identify remediable factors in the practice of anaesthesia, all types of surgery and now invasive procedures. Data are supplied on a voluntary basis; consultant clinicians in the relevant specialties are invited to participate. NCEPOD also reviews requests for and reporting of postmortem examinations.

The Enquiry collects information on deaths in hospital within 30 days of an invasive procedure involving local, regional or general anaesthetic or sedation. Maternal deaths are not included in the Enquiry (they are covered by the Confidential Enquiry into Maternal Deaths).

Reporting of deaths

NCEPOD depends on local reporters to provide data on deaths in their hospital(s). Most of the reporters in the public sector are consultant clinicians who have devised their own methods of obtaining the information; many have delegated the data collection to administrative staff. In the independent sector, hospital or nursing managers provide the data. When incomplete information is received, the NCEPOD staff contact the appropriate medical records or information officer or secretarial or clinical audit staff.

Reporters provide the following information, which is entered onto the computer database:

> Name of authority/trust
> Name/sex/hospital number of patient
> Name of hospital in which the death occurred (and hospital where surgery took place, if different)
> Date of birth, final operation and death
> Surgical procedure performed
> Name of consultant surgeon
> Name of anaesthetist

The data collection year runs from 1 April to 31 March.

Sample for more detailed review

The nature of the sample changes annually, agreed before the start of the data collection. Information about a selected number of deaths is obtained by means of questionnaires. These are sent to consultant clinicians who are also asked to provide photocopies of relevant parts of the patient's notes (see "Confidentiality" below).

NCEPOD may collect data about patients who have survived more than 30 days after a procedure. These data are used for comparison with the data about deaths, or to review a specific aspect of clinical practice. Data from other sources may also be used.

Clinical Coordinators

The Trustees, on the recommendation of the Steering Group, appoint for a defined tenure Clinical Coordinators who lead the review of the data relating to the annual sample and advise the Steering Group and the Trustees.

They may also from time to time appoint Assistant Clinical Coordinators, who must be engaged in active academic/clinical practice (in the NHS) during the full term of office.

Advice

The Clinical Coordinators obtain advice from consultant clinicians in current practice. The Steering Group recommends the method of selection of these advisors.

Analysis and review of data

The collection, recording and analysis of data are managed by the Chief Executive of NCEPOD.

Reports

NCEPOD publishes a report which includes aggregated data and commentary on the information received. The reports are prepared by the Clinical Coordinators, Chief Executive and administrative staff and are reviewed in detail and approved by the Steering Group before publication.

General recommendations are made as well as specific points for individual specialties. Reports may include, as acknowledgements, the names of consultant clinicians who have returned questionnaires and whose names are known to NCEPOD.

Confidentiality

NCEPOD is registered with the Data Protection Registrar and abides by the Data Protection Principles. NCEPOD does not provide individual data to any person or organization outside the NCEPOD staff, coordinators, Trustees and Steering Group other than in the published Report.

All reporting forms, questionnaires and other paper records relating to the sample are shredded once an individual report has been published. Similarly, all patient-related data are removed from the computer database.

Data in the reports are aggregated to regional or national level so that individual Trusts, hospitals, authorities and patients and clinicians (who treat them) cannot be identified.

Before review of questionnaires by the Clinical Coordinators or any of the advisors, all identification is removed from the questionnaires and accompanying papers. The source of the information is not revealed to any of the Coordinators or advisors.

---End----

Appendix E - General data 1996/97

Reporting of deaths

Local reporters (see Appendix L) provided data to NCEPOD about patients who died in hospital between 1 April 1996 and 31 March 1997 within 30 days of a surgical procedure. We were also informed of a few deaths which occurred at home within the 30-day period.

Tables G1 to G4 refer to the total number of 19496 reported deaths. This total does not include nine reports where, despite all efforts, the data were incomplete, 168 reports received too late for inclusion in the analysis, and 969 inappropriate reports (see table G5). The regional breakdown of total deaths reported to NCEPOD, together with the totals of reports for previous years, are shown in table G1. The year-on-year fluctuations are in part caused by local (hospital) problems with data collection, and changes in the regional structure of the NHS. This means that the figures for years before 1996/97 are not directly comparable with those for earlier years.

Table G1
Deaths reported to NCEPOD

				Previous years				
	1996/97	1995/96	1994/95	1993/94	1992/93	1991/92	1990	1989
Anglia & Oxford	**1578**	1672	1361	1577	1862	1556	1367	1371
North Thames	**2292**	2081	1944	2703	2515	2127	2554	2609
North West	**2634**	2736	2618	2636	2378	2509	2736	2864
Northern & Yorkshire	**2870**	3110	2549	2637	2671	2267	2464	2685
South & West	**2201**	2508	2469	2561	2493	1847	1997	2306
South Thames	**2330**	2166	2246	2531	2445	2465	2457	2840
Trent	**2218**	2397	2386	2342	2036	2014	1722	1849
West Midlands	**1527**	1595	1531	1578	1565	1578	1826	1902
Wales	**1102**	840	933	1078	1072	1079	1102	1162
Northern Ireland	**480**	469	497	529	474	375	316	380
Guernsey	**27**	33	12	33	26	18	39	32
Jersey	**18**	26	17	27	32	25	22	26
Isle of Man	**26**	0	0	25	41	25	25	7
Defence Medical Services	**8**	7	17	36	40	75	60	94
Independent sector	**185**	201	148	149	166	172	130	120
Total	**19496**	19841	18728	20442	19816	18132	18817	20247

Table G2
Calendar days from operation to death
(i.e. not 24 hour periods)

		%	
0 (i.e. day of operation)	2092	*10.7*	
1	2242	*11.5*	
2	1611	*8.3*	
3	1243	*6.4*	*36.9*
4	1090	*5.6*	
5	989	*5.1*	
6	893	*4.6*	
7	814	*4.2*	
8	753	*3.9*	*19.4*
9	686	*3.5*	
10	633	*3.2*	
11	598	*3.1*	
12	491	*2.5*	
13	496	*2.5*	*12.7*
14	436	*2.2*	
15	451	*2.3*	
16 to 20	1771	*9.1*	
21 to 25	1324	*6.8*	*20.4*
26 to 30	883	*4.5*	
Total	**19496**		

Figure G1 (see table G2)
Calendar days from operation to death
(i.e. not 24 hour periods)

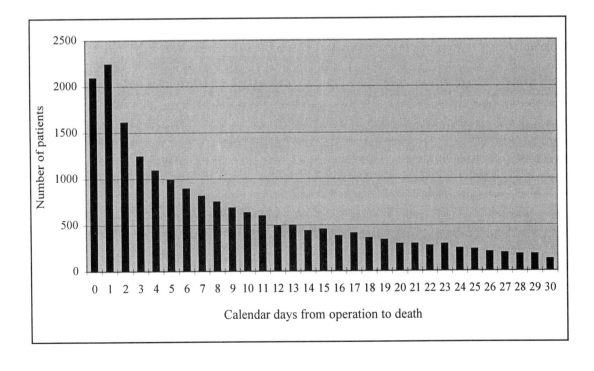

Table G3
Age/sex distribution of reported deaths

Age in years			Male	Female	Total
0	to	*4	129	94	223
5	to	9	16	7	23
10	to	14	16	13	29
15	to	19	49	13	62
20	to	24	55	20	75
25	to	29	62	43	105
30	to	34	68	47	115
35	to	39	77	58	135
40	to	44	152	103	255
45	to	49	221	141	362
50	to	54	267	205	472
55	to	59	453	336	789
60	to	64	783	476	1259
65	to	69	1253	817	2070
70	to	74	1840	1334	3174
75	to	79	1775	1476	3251
80	to	84	1441	1792	3233
85	to	89	909	1539	2448
90	to	94	312	785	1097
95	to	99	50	241	291
100	+		6	22	28
Total			**9934**	**9562**	**19496**

* *i.e. day of birth to the day preceding the fifth birthday*

Table G4
Calendar days between death and receipt of report by NCEPOD
(i.e. not 24 hour periods)

1	to	29	4922
30	to	59	4144
60	to	89	2665
90	to	119	2240
120	to	149	1621
150	to	179	1142
180	or	more	2762
Total			**19496**

Table G5
Inappropriate reports received and not included

270	More than 30 days *(day of operation to day of death)*
247	Procedure not performed by a surgeon
239	Duplicate report
186	No surgical procedure performed or inappropriate procedure *(according to NCEPOD criteria)*
18	Procedure performed in non-participating hospital
5	Patient still alive (death wrongly reported)
4	Maternal death
969	**Total**

These figures do not include inappropriate reports included in computer printout format. Some hospital systems cannot easily filter out inappropriate reports such as deaths following procedures by physicians, or deaths following procedures excluded by NCEPOD.

Sample for detailed review

From a total of 19496 deaths reported to NCEPOD, the sample for this year comprised 2541 (13.0%) cases (see page 15 and Appendix A for details of the sample criteria)

Surgical questionnaires

Questionnaires were sent to consultant surgeons for further information on all 2541 cases, and 1808 completed questionnaires were returned to NCEPOD. The overall return rate (see table G6) was therefore 71.2% (1808/2541).

After excluding 111 questionnaires which were returned incomplete, related to the wrong operation or patient, or were returned too late to be included, 1697 questionnaires were analysed.

Anaesthetic questionnaires

Questionnaires were sent to consultant anaesthetists for further information on 1721 of the 2541 sample cases. No questionnaire was sent for the remaining 820 cases for the following reasons:

160   Name of appropriate consultant anaesthetist unobtainable or notified too late to send questionnaire
660   No anaesthetist involved *(local anaesthesia or sedation administered solely by the surgeon)*

Of the questionnaires distributed, 76.5% (1316/1721) were returned. After excluding 44 questionnaires which were returned incomplete, related to the wrong operation or patient, or were returned too late to be included, 1272 questionnaires were analysed.

Table G6
Distribution and return of questionnaires by NHS region

SQ = Surgical Questionnaire AQ = Anaesthetic Questionnaire	No. of Qs distributed		No. of Qs returned		% return rate		No. of Qs analysed		No. hospitals represented	
	SQ	AQ	SQ	AQ	SQ	AQ	SQ	AQ	SQ	AQ
Anglia & Oxford	188	132	152	109	80.9	82.6	141	106	23	23
North Thames	266	156	161	108	60.5	69.2	144	103	33	30
North West	391	274	274	186	70.1	67.9	255	179	36	33
Northern & Yorkshire	392	250	279	205	71.2	82.0	267	199	37	37
South & West	275	196	229	163	83.2	83.2	215	155	23	20
South Thames	266	165	177	122	66.5	73.8	168	120	25	26
Trent	329	235	228	177	69.3	75.3	215	170	18	18
West Midlands	176	135	122	103	69.3	76.3	119	101	21	19
Wales	137	97	95	74	69.3	76.2	85	72	16	16
Northern Ireland	85	47	62	38	72.9	80.9	59	37	14	10
Guernsey	5	5	5	4	100.0	80.0	5	4	1	1
Jersey	2	2	2	2	100.0	100.0	2	1	1	1
Isle of Man	4	3	3	2	75.0	66.7	3	2	1	1
Defence Medical Services	2	2	2	2	100.0	100.0	2	2	1	1
Independent sector	23	22	17	21	73.9	95.5	17	21	11	12
Total	**2541**	**1721**	**1808**	**1316**	**71.2**	**76.5**	**1697**	**1272**	**261**	**248**

It is pleasing to note that in the NHS, several regions/authorities achieved return rates of 80% or higher; there remains considerable room for improvement in the other regions and particularly in North and South Thames.

Table G7
Distribution and return of surgical questionnaires by sample group

	Number of cases in sample		Number of questionnaires returned		% questionnaires returned		Number of questionnaires analysed	
	SQ	AQ	SQ	AQ	*SQ*	*AQ*	SQ	AQ
Gynaecology	265	244	213	209	*80.4*	*85.7*	205	201
Head and neck surgery	466	335	346	238	*74.2*	*71.0*	315	229
Minimally invasive surgery	625	236	354	160	*56.6*	*67.8*	310	155
Oesophageal surgery	406	270	288	206	*70.9*	*76.3*	273	198
Spinal surgery	99	81	79	59	*79.8*	*72.8*	76	57
Urology	680	555	528	444	*77.6*	*80.0*	518	432
Total	**2541**	**1721**	**1808**	**1316**	*71.2*	*76.5*	**1697**	**1272**

Table G8
Reasons for the non-return of questionnaires

Surgical Questionnaires	Anaesthetic Questionnaires	
459	263	No reason given
102	85	Medical notes lost or unavailable
114	21	Surgeon/anaesthetist judged return of questionnaire 'inappropriate'
27	24	Surgeon/anaesthetist no longer working at the hospital or on sick-leave
7	2	Consultant did not wish to participate
24	10	Other
733	**405**	**Total**

Selected data from the completed anaesthetic and surgical questionnaires

Table G9 (q59 – surgical questionnaire)
Has this death been considered (or will it be considered) at a local audit/quality control meeting and/or was a postmortem examination performed?

	PM + audit	PM only	Audit only	Neither	**Total**
Gynaecological surgery	21	32	47	105	**205**
Head and neck surgery	61	23	106	125	**315**
Minimally invasive surgery	64	14	152	80	**310**
Oesophageal surgery	63	11	156	43	**273**
Spinal surgery	24	9	24	19	**76**
Urological surgery	124	28	243	123	**518**
Total	**357**	**117**	**728**	**495**	**1697**

Table G10 (q67a – anaesthetic questionnaire)
Do you have morbidity/mortality review meetings in your department?

Yes	1171
No	92
Not answered	9
Total	**1272**

If yes, will this case be or has it been discussed at your departmental meeting?

Yes	345
No	802
Not answered	11
Not known/not recorded	13
Total	**1171**

Although 64% of these deaths were considered at a surgical audit meeting, only 29% were discussed at an anaesthetic departmental meeting. In 7% of returned questionnaires it was stated that there was no anaesthetic morbidity/mortality review meeting at which such discussion could have taken place.

NATIONAL CONFIDENTIAL ENQUIRY INTO PERIOPERATIVE DEATHS

35-43 Lincoln's Inn Fields, London, WC2A 3PN

ANAESTHETIC QUESTIONNAIRE 1996/97

QUESTIONNAIRE No.   **A**

DO NOT PHOTOCOPY ANY PART OF THIS QUESTIONNAIRE

QUESTIONNAIRE COMPLETION

This questionnaire should be completed with reference to the final operation before the death of the patient specified by NCEPOD. If you feel that this was not the **main** operation in the period before the patient's death, please give additional information.

Please **enclose** a copy of the ANAESTHETIC RECORD and of the FLUID BALANCE CHARTS. These are especially important. Any identification will be removed in the NCEPOD office.

All original copies of correspondence with NCEPOD are confidential (**but do not retain copies of your correspondence**).

The whole questionnaire will be shredded when data collection is complete.

For further information or for assistance, please contact the NCEPOD office on:

Tel: 0171 831 6430
Fax: 0171 430 2958

HAVE YOU ENCLOSED COPIES OF THE ANAESTHETIC RECORD AND FLUID BALANCE CHARTS?

Please use this section to provide extra information to help the advisory group of anaesthetists to understand aspects of this case which may not be apparent from your answers to the questions. The advisors who read this questionnaire are not apportioning blame. NCEPOD enquires into clinical practice in order to identify remediable factors in the practice of anaesthesia. It is intended to help clinicians to improve the care of patients.

Please write clearly, and ensure the accuracy of the information given.

PROXY ANAESTHETISTS

1 If you were not involved in any way with this anaesthetic and have completed the questionnaire on behalf of someone else, please indicate your position.

- **A** Chairman of Division ☐ 1
- **B** College tutor — 3a
- **C** Duty consultant — 3b
- **D** Other consultant
- **E** Other (please specify) _____ 4

THE ANAESTHETISTS

We want to know about the experience of this **most senior anaesthetist** in the operating room at the start of this procedure.

Questions 3 to 7 inclusive refer to **this** anaesthetist.

2 What was the grade of the **most senior anaesthetist** present at the **start** of the anaesthetic?
Please enter the appropriate letter in the box. ☐ 2

Trainee grade and years of training*

- **A** Senior house officer - Year 1
- **B** Senior house officer - Year 2
- **C** Senior house officer - more than two years
- **D** Specialist registrar - Year 1
- **E** Specialist registrar - Year 2
- **F** Specialist registrar - Year 3
- **G** Specialist registrar - Year 4
- **H** Specialist registrar - Accredited/CCST
- **I** Other trainee - please specify

Career grades

- **J** Consultant
- **K** Staff grade
- **L** Associate specialist

Other grades

- **M** General practitioner
- **N** Hospital practitioner
- **O** Other (please specify)

* this is designed as if the Calman proposals were in place. If there is a delay in implementation, please complete the question as if the changes had taken place.

3 Year of **primary** medical qualification [1][9][ ][ ] 3a

Please state country in which medical qualification awarded _____ 3b

4 Year of first full-time anaesthetic training post [1][9][ ][ ] 4

5 Which **higher diploma(s)** in **anaesthesia** were held at the time of the operation?

		Year of award
A	None	☐
B	Fellowship (Royal College, College or Faculty)	☐ [1][9][ ][ ] 5b
	(please state country) _____	
C	DA (or Part 1 FRCA)	☐ [1][9][ ][ ] 5c
D	Part 2 FRCA (physiology/pharmacology)	☐ [1][9][ ][ ] 5d
E	Other (please specify)	☐ [1][9][ ][ ] 5e

6 If the most senior anaesthetist present at the start of the anaesthetic was not in a training grade, please enter the appropriate letters for weekly (i.e. more than 50 operations per year) NHS commitments in anaesthesia for the following:

- **A** Cardiac surgery [ ][ ][ ] 6
- **B** Children under 3 years old
- **C** Neurosurgery
- **D** None of the above

7 If the most senior anaesthetist at the start of the anaesthetic was not a consultant, where was consultant help available?

- **A** A consultant came to the theatre before the end of the anaesthetic ☐ 7
- **B** A consultant was available in the operating suite but not directly involved
- **C** A consultant was available in the hospital, but was not present in the operating suite
- **D** A consultant was available by telephone
- **E** Other (please specify) _____

THE PATIENT

10   Date of patient's birth   ☐☐ ☐☐ ☐☐   10
      D D   M M   Y Y

11   Date of admission to the hospital in which the final operation took place   ☐☐ ☐☐ ☐☐   11
      D D   M M   Y Y

12   Time of admission to that hospital   ☐☐☐☐   12
      (use 24 hour clock)

13   Was the patient transferred **as an inpatient** from another hospital?

   A   Yes   ☐   13a
   B   No

If yes, please explain the reason(s) _____

If yes, had the patient's condition apparently deteriorated during transfer?

   A   Yes   ☐   13b
   B   No

If yes, please explain _____

THE OPERATION

14   Please list any related surgical procedures carried out **prior** to this final operation.

Procedure _____ Date _____

_____

Please enclose a copy of the anaesthetic records for these operations.

15   What was the primary pre-operative diagnosis and **planned** final operation?

_____

_____

---

8   Grades of **other anaesthetists** present during the procedure.

Please enter the appropriate letter(s) for the anaesthetist(s) present at the start of or during the procedure, excluding the anaesthetist mentioned in question 2. If there **was** more than one anaesthetist of the same grade, please enter the same letter for each of these individuals.

	Start of anaesthetic	Later in the procedure

Trainee grade and years of training*

A   Senior house officer - Year 1   ☐☐☐   ☐☐☐
B   Senior house officer - Year 2
C   Senior house officer - more than two years

D   Specialist registrar - Year 1   ☐☐☐☐   ☐☐☐☐☐
E   Specialist registrar - Year 2
F   Specialist registrar - Year 3
G   Specialist registrar - Year 4
H   Specialist registrar - Accredited/CCST   ☐   ☐

I   Other trainee - please specify

Career grades

J   Consultant   ☐☐☐   ☐☐☐
K   Staff grade
L   Associate specialist

Other grades

M   General practitioner   ☐☐☐   8a   ☐☐☐   8b
N   Hospital practitioner
O   Other (please specify)

* this is designed as if the Calman proposals were in place. If there is a delay in implementation, please complete the question as if the changes had taken place.

9   Was **advice sought**, at any time, from another anaesthetist who was not present in the theatre at any time during the anaesthetic?

   A   Yes   ☐   9
   B   No

If yes, from whom was advice sought?

_____

16 Co-existing medical diagnoses at the time of the final operation. Please enter the appropriate letter in a box, and specify the disorder in the space next to the category.

| | | | | | | | | | | | | | | |

A
B
C
D
E
F
G
H
I
J
K
L
M
N
O

A none

B respiratory _____

C cardiac _____

D neurological _____

E endocrine _____

F alimentary _____

G renal _____

H hepatic _____

I musculoskeletal _____

J vascular _____

K haematological _____

L genetic abnormality _____

M obesity _____

N sepsis (specify site) _____

O other (please specify) _____

_____

17 What procedure(s) was **performed** (final operation)?

_____

_____

Please enclose a copy of the anaesthetic record and fluid balance chart(s).

18 NCEPOD classification of the final operation.

We ask you to take particular care with the answers to this question which are crucial to the analysis made by NCEPOD. Please note the specific definition of "Emergency".

☐ 18

A NCEPOD Emergency
B NCEPOD Urgent
C NCEPOD Scheduled
D NCEPOD Elective

NCEPOD Definitions - Classification of operation

Emergency

Immediate life-saving operation, resuscitation simultaneous with surgical treatment (e.g. trauma, ruptured aortic aneurysm). Operation usually within one hour.

Urgent

Operation as soon as possible after resuscitation (e.g. irreducible hernia, intussusception, oesophageal atresia, intestinal obstruction, major fractures). Operation usually within 24 hours.

Scheduled

An early operation, but not immediately life-saving (e.g. malignancy). Operation usually within 3 weeks.

Elective

Operation at a time to suit both patient and surgeon (e.g. cholecystectomy, joint replacement).

19 Was a record of the patient's weight available?

   A   Yes

   B   No

□ 19

If yes, what was this weight _____ kg

If no, the estimated weight was _____ kg

20 Was a record of the patient's height available?

   A   Yes

   B   No

□ 20

If yes, what was the height? _____ cm

If no, the estimated height was _____ cm

21 Was an anaesthetist **consulted by the surgeon** (as distinct from informed) before this operation?

   A   Yes

   B   No

□ 21

22 Did an anaesthetist visit the patient before the final operation?

   A   Yes

   B   No

□ 22

If no, why not? _____

If yes, where?

   A   Ward

   B   Outpatient department

   C   Accident and Emergency department

   D   ICU/HDU

   E   Other (please specify)

□ 22b

_____

If yes, was **this** anaesthetist present at the start of the final operation?

   A   Yes

   B   No

□ 22c

23 Which of the following **investigations** were done before the anaesthetic? This should include tests carried out in a referral hospital and for which the results were available before the final operation. Please enter the letter for each test.

Please write the results in the space next to the test name.

A	None	□ A
B	Haemoglobin	_____ gm.litre^{-1} □ B
C	Packed cell volume (haematocrit)	_____ □ C
D	White cell count	_____ x10^9.litre^{-1} □ D
E	Sickle cell test (eg Sickledex)	_____ □ E
F	Blood group +/- cross match	_____ □ F
G	Coagulation screen	_____ □ G
H	Plasma electrolytes Na	_____ m mol.litre^{-1} □ H
I	K	_____ m mol.litre^{-1} □ I
J	Cl	_____ m mol.litre^{-1} □ J
K	HCO$_3$	_____ m mol.litre^{-1} □ K 23
L	Blood urea	_____ m mol.litre^{-1} □ L
M	Creatinine	_____ micro mol.litre^{-1} □ M
N	Serum albumin	_____ g.litre^{-1} □ N
O	Bilirubin (total)	_____ micro mol.litre^{-1} □ O
P	Glucose	_____ m mol.litre^{-1} □ P
Q	Amylase	_____ □ Q
R	Urinalysis (ward or lab)	_____ □ R
S	Blood gas analysis	_____ □ S
T	Chest x-ray	_____ □ T
U	Electrocardiography	_____ □ U
V	Respiratory function tests	_____ □ V
W	Special cardiac investigation (eg cardiac catheterization)	_____ □ W
X	CAT scan/ultrasound/MRI/NMR	_____ □ X
Y	Special neurological investigation (eg imaging)	_____ □ Y
Z	Others relevant to anaesthesia (please specify)	_____ □ Z

_____

24 What drug(s) or other therapy was the patient receiving regularly at the time of operation (excluding premedication or drugs for anaesthesia)?

_____

_____

ASA GRADES

25 Please enter the patient's ASA status prior to the final operation. (NB we do not use the E subclassification). □ 25

Definitions of the ASA Grades

ASA 1 a normal healthy patient

ASA 2 a patient with mild systemic disease

ASA 3 a patient with severe systemic disease that limits activity but is not incapacitating

ASA 4 a patient with incapacitating systemic disease that is a constant threat to life

ASA 5 a moribund patient who is not expected to survive for 24 hours with or without an operation

PREPARATION OF THE PATIENT BEFORE THE OPERATION

26 Did the patient receive intravenous fluid therapy in the 12 hours before induction? □ 26

A Yes
B No

If yes, please send copies of the fluid balance charts.

27 Was it necessary to **delay** the anaesthetic to improve the patient's state before operation? □ 27a

A Yes
B No

If yes, please indicate which system(s) needed attention: □□□□□ 27b

A Cardiac

B Respiratory

C Metabolic

D Haematological

Please explain the reasons for the delay:

_____

_____

28 Were premedication drugs prescribed? □ 28

A Yes
B No

THE ANAESTHETIC

29 Time of start of anaesthetic
(enter "X" in boxes if times not recorded)   □□□□ 29
(use 24 hour clock)

30 Time of start of surgery   □□□□ 30
(use 24 hour clock)

31 Time of transfer out of operating room
(e.g. to recovery room, ICU)   □□□□ 31a
(use 24 hour clock)

If you are not able to provide the times, please indicate the total duration of the operation
(i.e. time of start of anaesthetic to time of transfer):   □□ hours □□ minutes 31b

32 What was the grade of the most senior **surgeon** in the operating room?

A House officer
B Senior house officer
C Specialist registrar
D Visiting registrar
E Associate specialist
F Clinical assistant
G Staff grade
H Consultant
I Other (please specify)

□ 32

33 Was there a trained anaesthetist's assistant (i.e. ODA, SODA, anaesthetic nurse) present for this case?   □ 33

A Yes
B No

If no, please explain

_____

_____

_____

34 Is there an anaesthetic record for this operation in the patient's notes?

☐ 34

A Yes
B No

If yes, please send a complete copy of it with this questionnaire to the NCEPOD office. (We will delete/ remove identification marks). The NCEPOD advisors cannot do their job effectively without this important record.

If no, please give as full an account as possible of the anaesthetic below. Please include details of anaesthetic agents, drugs, routes of administration, breathing systems and tube size.

_____
_____
_____
_____
_____
_____
_____
_____
_____
_____
_____
_____
_____
_____
_____
_____

FLUIDS DURING OPERATION

35 Did the patient receive intravenous fluids DURING the operation?

☐ 35

A Yes
B No

If yes, please indicate which:

	Fluid (indicate type by inserting appropriate letter)	Total volume during operation (mls)

Crystalloid

A Dextrose 5%
B Dextrose 4% saline 0.18%
C Dextrose 10%
D Saline 0.9%
E Hartmann's (compound sodium lactate)
F Other (please specify)

35a

Colloid (and others)

A Modified gelatin (Gelofusine, Haemaccel)
B Human albumin solution
C Starch (HES)
D Dextran
E Mannitol (Please specify concentration)
F Other (please specify)

35b

Blood

A Whole blood
B Platelets
C Fresh frozen plasma
D Other component (please specify)

35c

36 Was the anaesthetic room used for the induction of anaesthesia?

☐ 36

A Yes
B No

TYPE OF ANAESTHESIA

37 Were monitoring devices used during the management of this anaesthetic?

A Yes
B No ☐ 37a

If yes, were monitoring instruments already attached to the patient (i.e. from ICU or A&E)?

A Yes
B No ☐ 37b

Please enter appropriate letter(s) in the boxes for monitoring devices used:

	In place already	Used during induction	Used during op
A ECG			
B pulse oximeter			
C indirect BP			
D oesophageal or precordial (chest wall) stethoscope			
E O₂ analyser			
F inspired anaesthetic vapour analyser			
G expired CO₂ analyser			
H airway pressure gauge			
J ventilation volume			
K ventilation disconnect device			
L peripheral nerve stimulator			
M temperature (state site) ____			
N urine output			
P CVP			
Q direct arterial BP (invasive)			
R pulmonary arterial pressure			
S intracranial pressure			
T EEG/CFAM/evoked responses			
V other (please specify)			

37c

38 Did anything hinder full monitoring?

A Yes
B No ☐ 38

If yes, please specify (e.g. bilateral arm surgery, radiotherapy, skin pigmentation, inaccessibility, non-availability of monitors):

_____

_____

_____

39 What type of anaesthesia was used?

A general alone (40 to 46)
B local infiltration alone
C regional alone (47 to 48)
D general and regional (40 to 48)
E general and local infiltration (40 to 46)
F sedation alone (49 to 50)
G sedation and local infiltration (49 to 50)
H sedation and regional (47 to 50)

☐ 39

Please now answer the questions indicated in brackets, and then continue from question 51.

GENERAL ANAESTHESIA

40 Was a nasogastric tube in place before induction?

A Yes
B No ☐ 40a

If yes, was it

a) aspirated before induction?

A Yes
B No ☐ 40b

b) removed before induction?

A Yes
B No ☐ 40c

41 Was cricoid pressure used at induction of anaesthesia?

A Yes
B No ☐ 41

42 Was the patient formally given oxygen to breathe spontaneously before induction?

A Yes
B No ☐ 42

43 Were the lungs inflated with an oxygen-rich mixture before tracheal intubation?

A Yes
B No ☐ 43

44 Was suxamethonium given to facilitate tracheal intubation?

A Yes
B No ☐ 44

45 How was the airway established during anaesthesia?

- **A** face mask (with or without oral airway)
- **B** laryngeal mask
- **C** orotracheal intubation
- **D** nasotracheal intubation
- **E** endobronchial
- **F** tracheostomy
- **G** patient already intubated prior to arrival in theatre suite
- **H** other (please specify)

45 ☐☐☐☐☐☐☐☐

46 Were there any problems with airway maintenance or ventilation?

- **A** Yes
- **B** No

If yes, please explain

46 ☐

REGIONAL ANAESTHESIA

47 If the anaesthetic included a regional technique, which method was used?

- **A** epidural - caudal
- **B**   - lumbar
- **C**   - thoracic
- **D** interpleural
- **E** intravenous regional
- **F** cranial or peripheral nerve blocks (please specify _____)
- **G** plexus block (e.g. brachial, 3-in-1 block)
- **H** subarachnoid (spinal)
- **J** surface (e.g. for bronchoscopy)

47 ☐☐☐☐☐☐☐☐

48 Which agent was used? Please specify drug(s) and dosage(s):

- **A** local _____
- **B** narcotic _____
- **C** other (please specify) _____

48 ☐☐☐

SEDATION (as opposed to General Anaesthesia)

49 Which sedative drugs were given for this procedure (excluding premedication)?

- **A** inhalant
- **B** narcotic analgesic
- **C** benzodiazepine
- **D** sub-anaesthetic doses of IV anaesthetic drugs
- **E** other (please specify) _____

49 ☐☐☐☐☐

50 Was oxygen given during the operation?

- **A** Yes
- **B** No

50a ☐

If **yes**, for what reason?

- **A** routine
- **B** otherwise indicated (please specify indications)

50b ☐☐

51 Where did this patient go on leaving the operating room?

- **A** recovery area or room equipped and staffed for this purpose*
- **B** high dependency unit*
- **C** intensive care unit*
- **D** specialised ICU
- **E** ward
- **F** another hospital
- **G** other (please specify)
- **H** died in theatre

51 ☐

52 Were you unable at any time to transfer the patient into an ICU, HDU etc?

- **A** Yes
- **B** No

52 ☐

If yes, please explain

* DEFINITIONS

A **recovery area** is an area to which patients are admitted from an operating room, where they remain until consciousness is regained and ventilation and circulation are stable.

An **intensive care unit (ICU)** is an area to which patients are admitted for treatment of actual or impending organ failure, especially when mechanical ventilation is necessary.

A **high dependency unit (HDU)** is an area for patients who require more intensive observation, treatment and nursing care than can be provided on a general ward. It would not normally accept patients requiring mechanical ventilation, but could manage those requiring intensive monitoring.

RECOVERY ROOM

If the patient did not enter a recovery room (option A on question 51), please move to question 56.

53 Were monitoring devices used, or investigations carried out during the management of this patient in the recovery room?

- **A** Yes
- **B** No

[ ] 53

If yes, please indicate which monitors were used. Enter the letter(s) in each appropriate box:

- **A** ECG
- **B** pulse oximeter
- **C** indirect BP
- **D** oesophageal or precordial (chest wall) stethoscope
- **E** O_2 analyser
- **F** expired CO_2 analyser
- **G** airway pressure gauge
- **H** ventilation volume
- **J** ventilator disconnect device
- **K** peripheral nerve stimulator
- **L** temperature (state site) _____
- **M** urine output
- **N** CVP
- **P** direct arterial BP (invasive)
- **Q** blood gas analysis
- **R** pulmonary arterial pressure
- **S** intracranial pressure
- **T** cardiac output
- **V** other (please specify) _____

[ ] 53b

54 Time of transfer from recovery area:

[ ][ ][ ][ ] 54

(use 24 hour clock)

(enter "X" in boxes if not recorded)

55 Where did this patient go next (i.e. after the recovery room)?

- **A** ward
- **B** high dependency unit
- **C** intensive care unit
- **D** specialised ICU
- **E** home
- **F** another hospital
- **G** died in recovery area
- **H** other (please specify)

[ ] 55

---

56 Was controlled ventilation used postoperatively?

- **A** Yes
- **B** No

[ ] 56a

If **yes**, why?

- **A** routine management
- **B** respiratory inadequacy
- **C** cardiac inadequacy
- **D** control of intracranial pressure or other neurosurgical indications
- **E** part of the management of pain
- **F** poor general condition of patient
- **G** to allow recovery of body temperature
- **H** other reasons (please specify) _____

[ ] A
[ ] B
[ ] C
[ ] D 56b
[ ] E
[ ] F
[ ] G
[ ] H

CRITICAL EVENTS DURING ANAESTHESIA OR RECOVERY

57 Did any of the following events, which required specific treatment, occur during anaesthesia or immediate recovery (ie the first few hours after the end of the operation)?

A   Yes

B   No

☐ 57a

If **yes**, please specify nature by insertion of the appropriate letter(s) in a box.

A   air embolus

B   airway obstruction

C   anaphylaxis

D   arrhythmia

E   bradycardia (to or less than 50% of resting)

F   bronchospasm

G   cardiac arrest (unintended)

H   convulsions

I   disconnection of breathing system

J   hyperpyrexia (greater than 40°C or very rapid increase in temperature)

K   hypertension (increase of more than 50% resting systolic)

L   hypotension (decrease of more than 50% resting systolic)

M   hypoxaemia (please state oxygen saturation)

N   misplaced tracheal tube

O   pneumothorax

P   pulmonary aspiration

Q   pulmonary oedema

R   respiratory arrest (unintended)

S   tachycardia (increase of 50% or more)

T   unintentional delayed recovery of consciousness

U   ventilatory inadequacy

V   excessive spread of regional anaesthesia (eg total spinal, overextensive epidural)

W   wrong dose or overdose of drug

X   other (please specify)

☐☐☐☐☐☐☐☐☐☐☐☐☐☐☐☐☐☐☐☐☐☐☐☐ 57b
A B C D E F G H I J K L M N O P Q R S T U V W X

Please specify location of patient, treatment and outcome.

_____

_____

_____

_____

58 Was there any mechanical failure of equipment during anaesthesia or recovery?

A   Yes

B   No

☐ 58a

If **yes**, please specify:

A   equipment for IPPV

B   suction equipment

C   syringe drivers

D   infusion pump

E   instrumental monitor (please specify)

F   other (please specify)

☐☐☐☐☐☐ 58b
A B C D E F

If the patient died in the theatre please move to question 63

59 What were the complications or events after this operation?

Please enter a letter for each, and specify in the space below each category:

A   ventilatory problems (e.g. pneumonia, pulmonary oedema)   ☐ A

B   cardiac problems (e.g. acute LVF, intractable arrhythmias, post-cardiac arrest)   ☐ B

C   hepatic failure   ☐ C

D   septicaemia   ☐ D

E   renal failure   ☐ E   59

F   central nervous system failure (e.g. failure to recover consciousness, CVA etc.)   ☐ F

G   progress of surgical condition   ☐ G

H   electrolyte imbalance   ☐ H

I   haematological disorder/coagulopathy   ☐ I

J   other (please specify)   ☐ J

Please give an account of any adverse events during this period.

_____

_____

DEATH

60 Were drugs given in the first 48 hours after operation **for pain**?

A Yes
B No
☐ 60a

If **yes**, which drug type?

A opiate / opioid
B local analgesic
C non-steroidal analgesic
D general (inhaled) anaesthetic
E other (please specify)
☐☐☐☐☐ 60b
A B C D E

Which method / route?

A intramuscular injection
B oral
C rectal
D continuous intravenous infusion
E PCA (patient-controlled analgesia)
F continuous epidural
G PCEA (patient-controlled epidural analgesia)
H inhaled
I other (please specify)
☐☐☐☐☐☐☐☐☐ 60c
A B C D E F G H I

_____

61 Did complications occur as a result of these analgesic methods?

A Yes
B No
☐ 61

If **yes**, please specify

_____

62 Were other sedative/hypnotic or other drugs given?

A Yes
B No
☐ 62a

If **yes**, which?

A propofol
B midazolam
C other benzodiazepine
D other (please specify)
☐☐☐☐ 62b
A B C D

_____

63 Date of death:
☐☐ ☐☐ ☐☐ 63
D D M M Y Y

64 Time of death:
☐☐ ☐☐ 64
(use 24 hour clock)

65 Place of death:

A theatre
B recovery area
C intensive care unit
D high dependency unit
E ward
F home
G another hospital
H other (please specify)
☐ 65

_____

66 Cause of death:

_____

67 Do you have morbidity/mortality review meetings in your department?

A Yes
B No
☐ 67a

If **yes**, will this case be, or has it been discussed at your departmental meeting?

A Yes
B No
☐ 67b

68 Has a consultant anaesthetist seen and agreed this questionnaire?

A Yes
B No
C Not applicable (completed by consultant)
☐☐☐ 68
A B C

PLEASE CONTINUE ON TO NEXT PAGE

REMINDER

**Have you enclosed copies of the
anaesthetic record and fluid balance charts?**

**THANK YOU FOR TAKING THE TIME TO COMPLETE THIS
QUESTIONNAIRE**

**You are advised for legal reasons not to keep a copy of this questionnaire,
because a copy would form a part of the patient's medical record.
All material sent to NCEPOD is ultimately destroyed.**

Please return the questionnaire and accompanying papers
in the reply-paid envelope provided.

If you wish to inform the NCEPOD office of any other details of this case,
please do so on a separate sheet, but include the number of the questionnaire.

CONSULTANT ANAESTHETISTS ONLY

We would like to publish the names of all

consultants who have returned completed questionnaires.

Please help us by providing your initials and surname.

This page will be removed from the questionnaire on receipt.

Initials _____ Surname _____

NATIONAL CONFIDENTIAL ENQUIRY INTO PERIOPERATIVE DEATHS

35-43 Lincoln's Inn Fields, London, WC2A 3PN

SURGICAL QUESTIONNAIRE 1996/97

QUESTIONNAIRE No.   **S**

DO NOT PHOTOCOPY ANY PART OF THIS QUESTIONNAIRE

QUESTIONNAIRE COMPLETION

This questionnaire should be completed with reference to the last operation before the death of the patient specified by the NCEPOD office. If you feel that this was not the <u>main</u> operation in the period before the patient's death, you may give additional information.

The whole questionnaire will be shredded when data collection is complete. The information will be filed anonymously.

Neither the questions nor the choices for answers are intended to suggest standards of practice.

Please enclose a copy of all the relevant surgical operation notes, the postmortem examination report and the histology report if available. Any identification will be removed in the NCEPOD office.

Many of the questions can be answered by "yes" or "no". **Please insert a tick (✓) in the appropriate box.**

Where multiple choices are given, please insert the tick(s) in the appropriate box(es).

Where more details are requested for an answer, please write in **BLOCK CAPITALS.**

In case of difficulty, please contact the NCEPOD office on:

Tel: 0171 831 6430
Fax: 0171 430 2958

HAVE YOU ENCLOSED COPIES OF THE OPERATION NOTES, POSTMORTEM EXAMINATION NOTES AND THE HISTOLOGY REPORT?

PLEASE USE THIS SECTION TO PROVIDE A BRIEF SUMMARY OF THIS CASE, ADDING ANY COMMENTS OR INFORMATION YOU FEEL ARE RELEVANT. **(PLEASE WRITE CLEARLY FOR THE BENEFIT OF THE SPECIALIST GROUP WHO WILL BE REVIEWING THE QUESTIONNAIRE).**

IF YOU WISH TO INFORM THE NCEPOD OFFICE OF ANY FURTHER DETAILS OF THIS CASE, PLEASE DO SO ON A SEPARATE SHEET, QUOTING THE QUESTIONNAIRE NUMBER.

PATIENT DETAILS

1   Date of birth

     D D M M Y Y   1

2   Date of **final** operation

     D D M M Y Y   2

3   Sex   Male   a   3

          Female   b

What diagnosis was recorded in the notes at the time of admission?

_____

_____

_____

ADMISSION TO THE HOSPITAL
IN WHICH THE OPERATION TOOK PLACE

4   Date of admission:

     D D M M Y Y   4

5   Admission category:

   a   Elective - at a time agreed between patient and surgical service

   b   Urgent - within 48 hours of referral / consultation

   c   Emergency - immediately following referral / consultation

If **elective**, date placed on waiting list or entered into admission diary:

     D D M M Y Y   5a

6   What was the pathway for this admission?

   a   Transfer as an inpatient from another <u>acute</u> surgical hospital

   b   Transfer from another non-surgical hospital, nursing home etc.

   c   Referral from a General Medical or General Dental Practitioner

   d   Admission following a previous outpatient consultation (please state date of outpatient attendance)

     D D M M Y Y

   e   Admission via A&E department

   f   Other (please state)

_____

Yes ☐ / No ☐ 9

If **no**, what was the source of referral to the Consultant Surgeon?

a   A medical specialty (please specify) ☐ a
_____

b   Another surgical specialty (please specify) ☐ b
_____

c   Same surgical specialty (please state reason for referral) ☐ c 9a
_____

d   Other (please specify) ☐ d
_____

Date and time of transfer to surgical team undertaking operation.

Date [ ][ ] [ ][ ] [ ][ ]
       D D   M M   Y Y

Time [ ][ ][ ][ ] 9b
(use 24 hour clock)

Date of first consultation following referral:

[ ][ ] [ ][ ] [ ][ ] 9c
 D D   M M   Y Y

10   Was there any delay in either the referral or the admission of this patient?

Yes ☐ / No ☐ 10

If **yes**, please specify.
_____
_____
_____
_____

N.B. If the patient was transferred as an inpatient from another acute surgical hospital, i.e. option "a" in Q6, please answer Q7; otherwise go directly to Q8.

7   Type of referring hospital:

a   (District) General
b   University/Teaching
c   Surgical Specialty
d   Other Acute/Partly Acute   7
e   Community
f   Defence Medical Services
g   Independent
h   Other (please specify)

[a][b][c][d][e][f][g][h]
_____

Why was the patient transferred?
_____

Did the patient's condition deteriorate during transfer?

Yes ☐ / No ☐ 7a

If **yes**, please specify
_____
_____

PREOPERATIVE CARE

8   To what type of area was the patient **first** admitted in "your" hospital (i.e. in which the final operation took place)?

a   Surgical ward (including surgical specialties)
b   Gynaecological/Obstetric ward
c   Medical ward
d   Mixed medical/surgical ward
e   Geriatric ward
f   Admission ward   8
g   A&E holding area (or other emergency admission ward)
h   Day unit
i   Direct to theatre
j   ICU
k   Coronary care unit (CCU)
m   HDU
n   Other (please specify)

[a][b][c][d][e][f][g][h][i][j][k][m][n]
_____

11   Specialty of Consultant Surgeon in charge at the time of the final operation (pleas tick only one box).

| | | | | | | | | | | | | | | | | | | | | |
|a|b|c|d|e|f|g|h|i|j|k|l|m|n|o|p|q|r|s|t|u|

a   General
b   General with special interest in Paediatric Surgery
c   General with special interest in Urology
d   General with special interest in Vascular Surgery
e   General with special interest in Gastroenterology
f   General with special interest in Endocrinology
g   General with special interest in (please specify) _____
h   Accident and Emergency
i   Cardiac/Thoracic/Cardiothoracic
j   Gynaecology
k   Neurosurgery
l   Ophthalmology
m   Oral/Maxillofacial
n   Orthopaedic
o   Otorhinolaryngology
p   Paediatric
q   Plastic
r   Transplantation
s   Urology
t   Vascular
u   Other(please specify)

_____
_____

12   What was the grade of the most senior surgeon **consulted** before this operation?

| | | | | | | | | | | | | | | | | |
|a|b|c|d|e|f|g|h|i| |j|k|m|n|o|p|q|

a   House Officer
b   Senior House Officer - Year 1
c   Senior House Officer - Year 2
d   Specialist Registrar - Year 1
e   Specialist Registrar - Year 2
f   Specialist Registrar - Year 3
g   Specialist Registrar - Year 4
h   Specialist Registrar - Accredited/CCST
i   Visiting Specialist Registrar
j   Locum Appointment - Training (state grade)
k   Locum Appointment - Service (state grade)
m   Staff Grade
n   Clinical Assistant
o   Associate Specialist
p   Consultant
q   Other (please specify)
_____

13   Please state the working diagnosis by the most senior member of the surgical team;
(**PLEASE USE BLOCK CAPITALS**)

_____
_____
_____
_____
_____

14   What operation was proposed by the most senior member of the surgical team?
(**PLEASE USE BLOCK CAPITALS**)

_____
_____
_____

15   What was the immediate indication for the proposed operation?
(**PLEASE USE BLOCK CAPITALS**)

_____
_____
_____

16 Please enter the patient's ASA status prior to the final operation. (NB we do not use the E subclassification).

1	2	3	4	5

16

American Society Of Anesthesiology (A.S.A.) Classifications Of Physical Status

Definitions

ASA 1 a normal healthy patient

ASA 2 a patient with mild systemic disease.

ASA 3 a patient with severe systemic disease that limits activity but is not incapacitating.

ASA 4 a patient with incapacitating systemic disease that is a constant threat to life.

ASA 5 a moribund patient who is not expected to survive for 24 hours with or without an operation.

17 Were there any coexisting problems (**other than the main diagnosis**) at the time of this operation?

Yes ☐
No ☐ 17

If **yes**, please put a tick in each appropriate box and specify the disorder in the space provided.

a Malignancy _____
b Respiratory _____
c Cardiac _____
d Renal _____
e Haematological _____
f Gastrointestinal _____
g Vascular _____
h Sepsis _____
i Neurological _____
j Diabetes mellitus _____
k Other endocrine _____
m Musculoskeletal _____
n Psychiatric _____
o Alcohol-related problems _____
p Drug addiction _____
q Genetic abnormality _____
r Other (please specify) _____

a	b	c	d	e	f	g	h	i	j	k	m	n	o	p	q	r

17a

18 What precautions or therapeutic manoeuvres **were** undertaken preoperatively (excluding anaesthetic room management) to improve the patient's preoperative condition?

Enter a tick in each appropriate box.

a None
b Cardiac support drugs or anti-arrhythmic agents
c Gastric aspiration
d Intravenous fluids
e Correction of hypovolaemia
f Urinary catheterisation
g Blood transfusion
h Diuretics
i Anticoagulants
j Vitamin K
k Antibiotics (pre- or intraoperative)
m Bowel preparation (specify method used) _____
n Chest physiotherapy
o Oxygen therapy
p Airway protection (e.g. in unconscious patients)
q Tracheal intubation
r Mechanical ventilation
s Nutritional support
t Others (please specify) _____

a	b	c	d	e	f	g	h	i	j	k	m	n	o	p	q	r	s	t

18

19 Were any measures taken (before, during or after operation) to prevent venous thromboembolism?

Yes ☐
No ☐ 19

OPERATION

20 Please list any previous operations. Please send all relevant operation notes.

Operation	Date	Specialty and grade of operating surgeon
a		
b		
c		
d		

21 Date of decision to operate:

[ ][ ] [ ][ ] [ ][ ] [ ]   21
D D   M M   Y Y

22 What was the anticipated risk of death related to the proposed operation?

a   Not expected

b   Small but significant risk

c   Definite risk

d   Expected

[ ][ ][ ][ ]   a b c d   22

If death was **expected,** please specify the anticipated benefit of the operation.

_____

_____

_____

23 Were there any delays (between admission and surgery) due to factors other than clinical?

Yes [ ]
No [ ]   23

If **yes**, please specify:

_____

_____

24 Classify this operation (see definitions below and choose the category most appropriate to the case).

a   Emergency

b   Urgent

c   Scheduled

d   Elective

[ ][ ][ ][ ]   a b c d   24

Definitions

a   **Emergency**
Immediate life-saving operation, resuscitation simultaneous with surgical treatment (e.g. trauma, ruptured aortic aneurysm). Operation usually within one hour.

b   **Urgent**
Operation as soon as possible after resuscitation (e.g. irreducible hernia, intussusception, oesophageal atresia, intestinal obstruction, major fractures). Operation usually within 24 hours.

c   **Scheduled**
An early operation but not immediately life-saving (e.g. malignancy). Operation usually within 3 weeks.

d   **Elective**
Operation at a time to suit both patient and surgeon (e.g. cholecystectomy, joint replacement).

25 Time of start of operation:
(not including anaesthetic time)

[ ][ ] [ ][ ]   25

(use 24 hour clock)

Duration of operation (not including anaesthetic time):

_____ hrs   _____ mins

26 Which grades of surgeon were present in the operating room during the procedure?

a	House Officer	
b	Senior House Officer - Year 1	
c	Senior House Officer - Year 2	
d	Specialist Registrar - Year 1	
e	Specialist Registrar - Year 2	
f	Specialist Registrar - Year 3	
g	Specialist Registrar - Year 4	
h	Specialist Registrar - Accredited/CCST	
i	Visiting Specialist Registrar	
j	Locum Appointment - Training (state grade)	
k	Locum Appointment - Service (state grade)	
m	Staff Grade	
n	Clinical Assistant	
o	Associate Specialist	
p	Consultant	
q	Other (please specify)	

[boxes a–i] [boxes j–q]   26

27 What was the grade of the **most senior operating surgeon** (as distinct from surgeons present in an assisting or supervisory capacity)?

a	House Officer	
b	Senior House Officer - Year 1	
c	Senior House Officer - Year 2	
d	Specialist Registrar - Year 1	
e	Specialist Registrar - Year 2	
f	Specialist Registrar - Year 3	
g	Specialist Registrar - Year 4	
h	Specialist Registrar - Accredited/CCST	
i	Visiting Specialist Registrar	
j	Locum Appointment - Training (state grade)	
k	Locum Appointment - Service (state grade)	
m	Staff Grade	
n	Clinical Assistant	
o	Associate Specialist	
p	Consultant	
q	Other (please specify)	

[boxes a–i] [boxes j–q]   27

We want to know about the experience and qualifications of the **most senior operating surgeon**. (Questions 28 to 31)

28 Year of **primary** medical qualification

[1][9][ ][ ]   28

29 Year of first full-time surgical training post

[1][9][ ][ ]   29

30 Which **higher diploma(s) in surgery** were held at the time of the operation?

Year of award

A None   [ ]

B Part 1 of Fellowship   [ ]

C Fellowship (Royal College, College or Faculty)   [ ]

(please state country if not UK _____)

[1][9][ ][ ]

D MS/MD   [ ]   [1][9][ ][ ]

E Intercollegiate specialty diploma   [ ]

(please state which diploma _____)

F Other (please specify)   [ ]   [1][9][ ][ ]

_____

31 How long had this surgeon spent in **this grade** in **this specialty**?

_____ yrs   _____ mths

31a How many similar procedures had **THIS** surgeon performed **in the previous 12 months**? (If not known, please enter an estimate)

_____ procedures

32 If the most senior operator was not a consultant, was a more senior surgeon **immediately available, i.e. in the operating room/suite?**

Yes [ ]
No [ ]   32

If **yes**, please specify grade and location.

Grade _____

Location _____

33 Operation undertaken:
    (PLEASE USE BLOCK CAPITALS)

    _____

    N.B. PLEASE ENCLOSE A COPY OF THE OPERATION NOTES.

34 If the operation undertaken was different to that <u>proposed</u>, please explain.

    _____

35 Please state the diagnosis established at operation:
    (PLEASE USE BLOCK CAPITALS)

    _____

36 Were there any unanticipated intra-operative problems?

    Yes ☐
    No ☐   36

    If **yes**, please specify.

    _____

37 Was the procedure performed **SOLELY** under local anaesthetic or sedation **administered by the SURGEON?**

    Yes ☐
    No ☐   37

    If **yes**, which of the following were recorded during or immediately after the procedure?

    a Blood pressure
    b Pulse
    c ECG
    d Pulse oximetry
    e Other (please specify) _____
    f None

    ☐ a ☐ b ☐ c ☐ d ☐ e ☐ f   37a

38 Was the patient admitted to an ICU or HDU* immediately after leaving the theatre suite?

    a Intensive Care Unit
    b High Dependency Unit
    c Neither of the above

    ☐ a ☐ b ☐ c   38

38a If **neither**, was the patient admitted to an ICU or HDU after an initial period on a routine postoperative ward?

    a Intensive Care Unit
    b High Dependency Unit
    c Neither of the above

    ☐ a ☐ b ☐ c   38a

    If either **a** or **b**, after how many days postoperatively? _____ days

    If the patient was admitted to an ICU or HDU please answer questions 39 to 41.

    If the patient was not admitted to an ICU or HDU, please continue from question 42.

    * DEFINITIONS (as used by the Association of Anaesthetists of Great Britain and Ireland)

    Intensive Care Unit (ICU): an area to which patients are admitted for treatment of actual or impending organ failure, especially when mechanical ventilation is necessary.

    High Dependency Unit (HDU): an area for patients who require more intensive observation, treatment and nursing care than can be provided on a general ward. It would not normally accept patients requiring mechanical ventilation, but could manage those receiving invasive monitoring.

a Death
b Elective transfer to ward
c Pressure on beds
d Other (please specify)

[| | | |] a b 39 c d

40 Was the patient subsequently readmitted to an ICU/HDU?

Yes
No
[|] 40

If yes, please give details.

_____

_____

_____

41 If the patient's condition warranted an admission to an ICU/HDU, were you at any time unable to transfer the patient into an ICU/HDU within the hospital in which the surgery took place?

Yes
No
Condition did not warrant admission to ICU/HDU
[| |] a 41 b c

If yes, why?

_____

_____

_____

[| | | | | | | | | | | | | | | | | | | | | | | | | |] a b c d 42 e f g h i j k l m n o p q r s t u v w x y z

a Haemorrhage/postoperative bleeding requiring transfusion
b Upper respiratory obstruction
c Respiratory distress
d Generalised sepsis
e Wound infection/dehiscence
f Anastomotic failure
g Cardiac arrest
h Low cardiac output/other cardiac problems
i Hepatic failure
j Renal failure
k Endocrine system failure
l Stroke or other neurological problems
m Persistent coma
n Other organ failure (please specify) _____
o Problems with analgesia
p DVT
q Pulmonary embolus
r Fat embolus
s Orthopaedic prosthetic complication
t Pressure sores
u Peripheral ischaemia
v Urinary tract infection
w Urinary retention/catheter blockage
x Ureteric injury/fistula
y Nutritional problems
z Other(please specify)

43 Was there a shortage of personnel in this case?

Yes
No
[|] 43

If **yes**, which?

a Consultant surgeons
b Trainee surgeons
c Consultant anaesthetists
d Trainee anaesthetists
e Skilled assistants
f Nurses
g ODAs
h Porters
i Other (please specify) _____

[| | | | | | | | |] a b c d 43a e f g h i

DEATH

44 Date of death:

D D M M Y Y   44

45 Time of death:

(use 24 hour clock)   45

46 Place of death:

- a Theatre
- b Recovery room
- c Ward
- d ICU/HDU
- e CCU or other specialised ICU
- f Home
- g Another acute hospital
- h Other (please specify)

a b c d e f g h   46

47 Was cardiopulmonary resuscitation attempted?

Yes
No   47

If **no**, was this a decision made preoperatively?

Yes
No   47a

48 What was the immediate **clinical** cause of death (this need not be a duplication of the death certificate)?
(PLEASE USE BLOCK CAPITALS)

49 **CAUSE OF DEATH** (this is a facsimile of the death certificate: please complete it accordingly, using **BLOCK CAPITALS**).

I (a) Disease or condition directly leading to death

(b) Other disease or condition, if any, leading to I (a)

(c) Other disease or condition, if any, leading to I (b)

II Other significant conditions CONTRIBUTING TO THE DEATH but not related to the disease or condition causing it

50 Was the death reported to the Coroner?

Yes
No   50

If **yes**, was a Coroner's postmortem examination ordered and performed?

Yes
No   50a

If a Coroner's postmortem examination was performed, please answer questions 52 to 58.

51 If a Coroner's postmortem examination **was not** performed, was a hospital examination undertaken?

Yes
No   51

If **no**, why not?

N.B. If a postmortem examination was not performed, please move to question 59.

Yes   a ⬚
No   b ⬚   56
None received   c ⬚

If **no**, what was different?

_____

_____

57   Who performed the postmortem examination?

a   Consultant pathologist   a ⬚
b   Junior pathologist   b ⬚   57
c   Not known   c ⬚

58   Please specify the specialty of the pathologist who performed the postmortem examination.

a   General histopathologist   a ⬚
b   Home Office histopathologist   b ⬚
c   Neuropathologist   c ⬚   58
d   Paediatric pathologist   d ⬚
e   Non-histopathologist (eg. chemical pathologist)   e ⬚

    please specify _____

Yes ⬚
No ⬚   52

52a   If **yes**, which member of the surgical team attended the postmortem examination?

a   None
b   House Officer
c   Senior House Officer
d   Specialist Registrar   52a
e   Staff Grade
f   Clinical Assistant
g   Associate Specialist
h   Consultant
i   Other (please specify) _____

53   If a surgeon **did not** attend the postmortem examination, why not?

_____

_____

54   Did the surgical team receive a copy of the postmortem examination report?

Yes ⬚
No ⬚   54
Informal report or verbal message ⬚

54a   If **yes**, when was this received?

⬚⬚ ⬚⬚ ⬚⬚   54a
D D M M Y Y

55   Please list the relevant findings of the postmortem examination including histology.
(PLEASE USE BLOCK CAPITALS)

_____

_____

_____

_____

_____

_____

**PLEASE SEND A COPY OF ALL POSTMORTEM EXAMINATION REPORTS,
POSTMORTEM REQUEST FORM AND HISTOLOGY REPORTS IF AVAILABLE**

AUDIT

59 Has this death been considered, (or will it be considered) at a local audit/quality control meeting?

Yes ☐
No ☐ 59

60 Did you have any problems in obtaining the patient's notes (i.e. more than 1 week)?

Yes ☐
No ☐ 60

If **yes**, how long did they take to reach you? _____

61 Were all the notes available?

Yes ☐
No ☐ 61

If **no**, which part was inadequate/unavailable?

a Preoperative notes
b Operative notes
c Postoperative notes
d Death certificate book
e Nursing notes
f Anaesthetic notes
g Postmortem report
h Other notes (please specify) _____

☐☐☐☐☐☐☐☐ 61a
a b c d e f g h

62 Please state the <u>grade</u> of the surgeon who completed this questionnaire

_____

63 Has the consultant surgeon seen and agreed this questionnaire?

Yes ☐
No ☐ 63

64 Date questionnaire completed

☐☐ ☐☐ ☐☐ 64
D D M M Y Y

THANK YOU FOR TAKING THE TIME TO COMPLETE THIS QUESTIONNAIRE

<u>YOU MUST NOT KEEP A COPY OF THIS QUESTIONNAIRE</u>

Please return it in the reply-paid envelope provided to:

NCEPOD
35-43 Lincoln's Inn Fields
LONDON
WC2A 3PN

THIS QUESTIONNAIRE IS THE PROPERTY OF NCEPOD

Appendix H - Pathology proforma 1996/97

NCEPOD No.   **Type of autopsy**   ☐ Hospital   ☐ Coroner   ☐ Other

GENERAL FEATURES OF THE AUTOPSY REPORT

The report is typewritten   ☐ Yes   ☐ No

A clinical history is provided   ☐ Yes   ☐ No
When present the clinical history is
- ☐ 1 Unacceptably brief, obscure, uninformative
- ☐ 2 Poor
- ☐ 3 Satisfactory
- ☐ 4 Good
- ☐ 5 Fully detailed, clear, informative

A summary of lesions is present   ☐ Yes   ☐ No
When present this corresponds accurately to the text report   ☐ Yes   ☐ No

An OPCS cause of death is present   ☐ Yes   ☐ No
When present this corresponds accurately to the text report   ☐ Yes   ☐ No
When present this follows OPCS formatting rules   ☐ Yes   ☐ No

A clinico-pathological correlation is present   ☐ Yes   ☐ No
When present the clinico-pathological correlation is
- ☐ 1 Unacceptably brief, obscure, uninformative
- ☐ 2 Poor
- ☐ 3 Satisfactory
- ☐ 4 Good
- ☐ 5 Fully detailed, clear, informative

SPECIFIC FEATURES OF THE AUTOPSY REPORT

The description of external appearances is
- ☐ 1 Unacceptably brief, inadequately detailed
- ☐ 2 Poor
- ☐ 3 Satisfactory
- ☐ 4 Good
- ☐ 5 Fully detailed, clear, informative

Scars and incisions are measured   ☐ Yes   ☐ No   ☐ N/A

The gross description of internal organs is
- ☐ 1 Unacceptably brief, inadequately detailed
- ☐ 2 Poor
- ☐ 3 Satisfactory
- ☐ 4 Good
- ☐ 5 Fully detailed, clear, informative

Organs weighed (paired organs score 1)   ☐ 0   ☐ 1   ☐ 2   ☐ 3   ☐ 4   ☐ 5   ☐ 6   ☐ 7   ☐ 8   ☐ 9
The skull and brain have been examined   ☐ Yes   ☐ No
The operation site is described   ☐ Yes   ☐ No   ☐ N/A
The gross examination is appropriate to the clinical problem   ☐ Yes   ☐ No
Samples have been taken for:
- ☐ 1 Histology
- ☐ 2 Microbiology
- ☐ 3 Toxicology
- ☐ 4 Other
- ☐ 5 None of these

In my judgement samples should have been taken for:

☐ 1 Histology
☐ 2 Microbiology
☐ 3 Toxicology
☐ 4 Other
☐ 5 None of these

A histology report is included with the PM report
When present the histological report is:

☐ Yes   ☐ No
☐ 1 Unacceptably brief, inadequately detailed
☐ 2 Poor
☐ 3 Satisfactory
☐ 4 Good
☐ 5 Fully detailed, clear, informative

When absent does the lack of histology detract significantly from the value of this report?

☐ Yes   ☐ No

My overall score for this autopsy is:

☐ 1 Unacceptable, laying the pathologist open to serious professional criticism
☐ 2 Poor
☐ 3 Satisfactory
☐ 4 Good
☐ 5 Excellent, meeting all standards set by RCPath booklet

CLINICAL RELEVANCE

When the history, antemortem clinical diagnosis and cause of death are compared with the postmortem findings, this autopsy demonstrates (more than one answer will often apply):

☐ 1   A discrepancy in the cause of death or in a major diagnosis, which if known, might have affected treatment, outcome or prognosis

☐ 2   A discrepancy in the cause of death or in a major diagnosis, which if known, would probably not have affected treatment, outcome or prognosis

☐ 3   A minor discrepancy

☐ 4   Confirmation of essential clinical findings

☐ 5   An interesting incidental finding

☐ 6   A failure to explain some important aspect of the clinical problem, as a result of a satisfactory autopsy

☐ 7   A failure to explain some important aspect of the clinical problem, as a result of an unsatisfactory autopsy

ANY FEATURES WHICH MIGHT BE QUOTED IN THE NCEPOD REPORT:

Appendix J - Participants

Consultant anaesthetists

These consultant anaesthetists returned at least one questionnaire relating to the period 1 April 1996 to March 1997. We are not able to name <u>all</u> of the consultants who have done so as their names are not known to us.

Adams H.G.	Beers H.T.B.	Caddy J.M.	Cotton B.R.	Edge W.G.
Adley R.	Bembridge J.L.	Campbell N.	Counsell D.	Edmondson L.
Ahmed M.	Benedict M.	Campbell W.I.	Cowan P.	Edmondson R.S.
Aitkenhead A.R.	Bennett A.	Canton J.L.	Craddock S.C.	Edmondson W.C.
Akhtar M.	Bennett J.A.	Carlisle R.J.T.	Craig J.F.	Edwards A.E.
Akinpelu O.E.	Bennett S.R.	Carnie J.C.	Cranston D.	Edwards G.
Al Quisi N.K.S.	Berry C.	Carson D.	Creagh-Barry P.	Edwards H.
Al-Kassim N.	Bexton M.	Carter M.I.	Cross G.D.	El-Kholy M.
Al-Shaikh B.Z.	Bhaskar H.K.	Casey W.F.	Culbert B.	El-Rakshy M.
Alagesan K.	Biggart M.	Cash T.I.	Curran J.P.	Elliot J.M.
Albin M.Z.	Bird T.M.	Cashman J.N.	Cyna A.	Elliott D.J.
Alexander C.A.	Birks R.J.S.	Catling J.S.	Dann W.L.	Elliott R.H.
Allan D.J.	Bishton I.	Caunt J.A.	Darling R.	Elsworth C.
Amin S.	Blackburn A.	Chadwick I.S.	Dasey N.	Eltoft M.E.
Ammar T.A.A.	Blake D.	Chaffe A.G.	Daum R.E.O.	Eltringham R.J.
Anandanesan J.	Blogg C.E.	Challands J.	Davidson D.G.D.	Emam M.S.
Anderson J.	Bloor G.K.	Chalmers E.P.D.	Davies G.	Emery F.M.
Anderson J.D.	Blundell M.D.	Chamberlain M.E.	Davies J.R.	Emmanuel E.R.
Andrew D.S.	Boaden R.W.	Chambers J.J.	Davies K.J.	Enraght-Moony R.N.
Andrews C.J.H.	Boobyer M.D.	Chapman J.M.	Davies M.	Eppel B.
Andrews J.I.	Bousfield J.D.	Charters P.	Davies P.R.F.	Erskine R.
Ankutse M.	Bowley C.J.	Charway C.L.	Davies R.	Erwin D.C.
Antrobus J.H.L.	Bowman R.A.	Cheema S.	Davis I.	Evans C.S.
Appleby J.N.	Bowring D.	Chetty S.	Day S.	Evans G.
Aquilina R.	Boyd J.D.	Choudhry A.	de Courcy J.	Evans I.M.
Archer P.L.	Boyd T.	Chow A.E.	De Silva T.	Evans K.
Armstrong J.	Boyd V.	Christian A.S.	Dearden N.M.	Evans R.J.C.
Arnold R.W.	Boyle A.S.	Chung R.A.	Desborough R.C.	Ewart M.C.
Arrowsmith A.E.	Brampton W.	Chung S.K.N.	Deulkar U.V.	Fahy L.T.
Ashby M.W.	Bramwell R.G.B.	Church J.J.	Devine A.	Fairbrass M.J.
Ashurst N.H.	Bray B.M.	Clark G.	Dewar J.A.	Farling P.A.
Aspbury J.N.	Breen D.P.	Clarke K.	Dhariwal N.K.	Farquharson S.
Astley B.A.	Brice D.D.	Clayton K.C.	Dickson D.E.	Ferguson M.R.
Ather T.	Brighouse D.	Clunie R.W.D.	Dixon J.	Fergusson N.V.
Atkinson R.E.	Brighten P.W.	Coad N.	Dobson M.B.	Field L.
Auterson T.	Brim V.B.	Cobner P.G.	Dodds C.	Firn S.
Avery A.F.	Bristow A.S.E.	Cockroft S.	Doran B.R.H.	Fleming B.G.
Baichoo S.	Broadley J.	Cody M.	Dormon F.M.	Fletcher S.J.
Bailey C.R.	Brodrick P.M.	Coe A.J.	Dowdall J.W.	Flynn M.J.
Bailey D.M.	Brooker J.	Coghill J.C.	Dowling R.M.	Fogarty D.
Bailey P.W.	Brooks A.M.	Cohen D.G.	Doyle L.	Ford P.
Baker G.M.	Brooks R.J.	Cole J.R.	Drummond R.S.	Forster D.M.
Balakrishnan P.H.	Brown C.	Collis R.	Du Boulay P.M.	Forward R.
Baldwin L.N.	Brown J.G.	Colville L.J.	Dua R.	Francis G.A.
Ballance P.G.	Brown J.J.	Conway M.	Duggan J.E.	Francis R.I.
Ballard P.K.	Brown R.	Conyers A.B.	Duncan N.H.	Frater R.A.S.
Balmer H.G.R.	Brownlie G.	Cook L.B.	Dunn S.R.	Freeman J.
Bansal O.P.	Brunner M.D.	Cook M.H.	Dunnet J.	Freeman R.
Bardgett D.M.M.	Bryan G.	Cook P.R.	Dunnett I.A.R.	Frew R.M.
Bardosi L.	Bryant J.D.	Cooper A.E.	Duthie D.J.R.	Frimpong S.
Basu S.	Buckland R.W.	Cooper A.R.	Dwyer N.	Frost A.R.
Baxter R.C.H.	Buist R.J.	Cooper P.D.	Dyar O.	Fuzzey G.J.J.
Bayoumi M.	Bull P.T.	Coote M.J.A.	Earnshaw G.	Gabbott D.A.
Beck G.N.	Burchett K.R.	Coren A.	Eatock C.R.	Gabrielczyk M.R.
Beechey A.P.G.	Burns A.	Cotter J.	Eddleston J.M.	Gademsetty M.K.

Gadgil P.S.
Galizia E.J.
Gallagher L.B.S.
Ganado A.
Ganepola S.R.
Gardner L.G.
Garrett C.P.O.
Gaston J.H.
Gavin N.J.
Gell I.R.
Gerrish S.P.
Ghandour F.M.
Ghattas B.F.A.
Ghazala J.
Ghosh N.
Ghosh S.
Gilbertson A.A.
Gill N.
Gill S.S.
Gillbe C.
Glew R.
Goldberg P.
Goldhill D.
Goodall J.R.
Goodrum D.T.
Goodwin A.P.E.
Goodwin A.P.L.
Goold J.E.
Gothard J.W.W.
Gough M.B.
Goulden P.
Goulding S.
Govenden V.
Graham S.
Grant I.C.
Gray A.J.G.
Gray B.M.
Gray D.
Gray S.
Green B.
Green C.P.
Green J.D.
Greenbaum R.
Greenwell S.K.
Greenwood B.K.
Greiff J.
Greig A.J.
Grieff J.
Griffiths R.
Groves J.
Grummitt R.
Gupta A.
Gwinnutt C.L.
Hackett G.H.
Hamilton-Farrell M.R.
Hampson J.M.
Handy J.L.
Hardwick P.B.
Hardy I.
Hargreaves C.G.
Hargreaves R.
Harmer M.
Harper J.
Harris C.
Harris D.N.F.
Harris G.
Harris T.J.B.

Harrison C.A.
Harrison G.R.
Harrison K.M.
Hartley M.
Harvey D.C.
Harvey P.B.
Hasbury C.R.
Haslett W.H.K.
Hawkins D.J.
Hawkins T.J.
Haycock J.C.
Hebden M.W.
Hegarty J.E.
Hegde R.T.
Heidelmeyer C.F.
Heining M.P.D.
Henderson P.A.L.
Heneghan C.P.H.
Hett D.
Higgins D.J.
Hill S.
Hitchings G.M.
Hoad D.J.
Hobbs G.
Hodgson R.M.H.
Holdcroft A.
Hollis J.N.
Hopkinson J.M.
Hopkinson R.B.
Howard R.P.
Howell R.S.C.
Howes D.
Howie J.
Huddy N.C.
Hughes J.
Hughes J.A.
Hughes T.J.
Hull J.
Hunsley J.E.
Hunter S.J.
Hurwitz D.S.
Huss B.K.D.
Hutchings P.J.G.
Hutchinson A.
Hutchinson H.T.
Hutchinson S.E.
Hutter C.
Hutton D.S.
Imrie M.M.
Inglis M.S.
Iyer D.
Jackson D.G.
James P.
James R.H.
Jamieson J.R.
Jappie A.G.
Jardine A.D.
Jarvis A.P.
Jasani A.
Jash K.
Javed E.B.
Jeffs S.
Jellicoe J.A.
Jenkins B.J.
Jephcott G.
Jeyapalan I.
Jeyaratnam P.

Jingree M.
Johnson C.J.H.
Johnson R.C.
Johnston J.R.
Johnstone R.D.
Jones D.I.
Jones K.E.
Jordan M.J.
Judkins K.
Kalia P.
Kay P.M.
Keane T.K.
Keeler J.
Keep P.J.
Kelly D.R.
Kelly E.P.
Kendall A.P.
Kenny N.T.
Keogh B.F.
Kerr J.H.
Kesseler G.
Kestin I.G.
Khalil H.R.I.
Khan M.Y.
Kilpatrick S.M.
King M.
King T.A.
Kipling R.M.
Kneeshaw J.
Knibb A.A.
Knights D.
Knowles M.G.
Kocan M.
Koehli N.
Kokri M.S.
Kong K.L.
Kotting S.C.
Kouzel A.S.
Kraayenbrink M.A.
Kumar V.
Lahoud G.
Lake A.P.J.
Lamb A.S.T.
Landon K.
Langham B.T.
Lanham P.R.W.
Lassey P.D.
Lavies N.G.
Laxton A.G.P.
Leach A.
Leach A.B.
Leadbeater M.J.
Leigh J.
Leigh J.M.
Leith S.
Lenoir R.
Lesser P.J.A.
Levitt M.J.
Levy D.
Lewis G.A.
Lewis M.A.H.
Lewis R.P.
Liddle M.
Lilburn J.K.
Lindop M.J.
Lindsay R.G.
Lindsay W.A.

Linsley A.
Linter S.P.K.
Lintin D.J.
Littler C.
Loh L.
Longan M.A.
Loveday R.
Lowry K.G.
Ludgrove T.
Lung C.P.C.
Luntley J.B.
Lynch L.
Macartney I.D.
McBride R.J.
McCallum I.J.
McCaughey W.
McCleane G.
McCluskey A.
McCrirrick A.
McCulloch D.A.
McDonnell J.
McEwen A.W.
McGeachie J.F.
McGuinness C.
McHugh P.
McHutchon A.
MacIntosh K.C.
Mackenzie S.I.P.
McKinnon P.
McLaren I.M.
Maclaurin R.E.
McLeod G.F.
McPherson J.J.
McSwiney M.
McVey F.
Madej T.H.
Magee P.T.
Maher O.A.
Mahoney A.
Mahroo A.R.
Male C.G.
Marjot R.
Marsh R.H.K.
Martin A.J.
Martin J.W.
Martin P.
Martin V.
Mason J.S.
Mason R.A.
Masri Z.
Masters A.P.
Matheson H.A.
Mathew P.
Mathias I.M.J.
Mathur N.K.
Matson A.M.
Matthews A.J.
Matthews R.F.J.
Mawson P.J.
Mayall R.M.
Mayor A.H.
Maz S.
Mazumder J.K.
Meadows D.P.
Melville C.
Mendel L.
Mercer N.P.

Metias V.F.
Mettam I.
Michael W.
Middleton C.M.
Mikl B.
Millican D.L.
Milne B.R.
Milne L.A.
Mishra K.P.
Mitchell R.G.
Mitchell R.W.D.
Monks P.S.
Moon C.J.
Moore J.K.
Moore K.C.
Morgan C.J.
Morgan M.
Morgan R.
Morris S.
Morriss G.W.
Mostert M.J.
Mowbray M.J.
Mudie L.L.
Muirhead R.
Mulholland D.
Mulrooney P.
Mulvein J.T.
Murphy J.
Murphy P.
Murray J.M.
Myatt J.K.
Myint Y.
Nalliah R.S.C.
Nandakumar C.G.
Nandi K.
Nash J.
Nash P.J.
Nathanson M.H.
Navaratnarajah M.N.
Naylor A.F.
Neasham J.
Newby D.M.
Newman V.J.
Newnam P.T.F.
Newson C.
Newton D.E.F.
Nicholl A.D.J.
Nickalls R.
Noble H.
Noble J.
Nolan J.
Norman J.
Normandale J.P.
Norton A.C.
Nunn G.F.
O'Connor M.
O'Donoghue B.
O'Donovan N.P.
O'Dwyer J.
O'Keefe V.
O'Riordan J.A.
O'Shea P.J.
Oduro-Dominah A.
Okonkwo N.
Orton J.K.
Osborne M.A.
Padfield A.

Pais W.A.	Rebstein S.E.	Segath M.	Tannett P.G.	Wark K.J.
Palin P.H.	Reddy B.K.	Seingry D.	Tarr T.J.	Waters J.H.
Panch G.	Redman D.R.O.	Sellwood W.G.	Tatham P.F.	Watkins T.G.
Papas S.	Redman L.R.	Seymour A.H.	Taylor C.	Watson D.M.
Pappin J.C.	Reed P.A.	Shah H.	Taylor M.	Watson N.A.
Park W.G.	Reeder M.	Shah M.M.	Teasdale A.	Watson-Jones E.
Parker C.J.R.	Reid M.F.	Shah R.K.	Tehan B.	Watt J.W.H.
Parmar N.	Reilly C.S.	Shah Z.P.	Telford R.	Watt T.
Parnell C.J.	Remington S.A.M.	Shakir S.A.	Thomas A.N.	Weller R.
Parry H.M.	Renshaw A.J.N.	Shambrook A.S.	Thomas D.G.	West K.J.
Parsloe M.	Renshaw V.	Shammas R.	Thomas S.	West S.
Patel R.	Restall J.	Sharawi R.	Thompson A.R.	Westbrook J.
Pathiratne L.S.I.	Rich P.	Sharpe T.D.E.	Thompson E.M.	Weston G.A.
Paul S.	Richards D.C.	Sharples A.	Thompson J.F.W.	Wheatley R.G.
Peacock J.E.	Richards E.	Shaw D.	Thomson J.	Whelan E.
Pearson R.M.G.	Richardson J.	Shaw T.C.	Thomson S.	White D.
Peden C.	Richmond M.N.	Sherry K.M.	Thomson W.	White D.J.K.
Peebles D.J.	Riddell G.S.	Short S.	Thorn J.L.	White M.J.
Pennefather S.H.	Ridley S.	Sides C.A.	Thorniley A.	White W.D.
Pepperman M.L.	Riedel B.	Silk J.M.	Thornley B.	Whitehead E.M.
Pereira N.H.	Rimell P.J.	Simpson D.A.	Till C.	Whittle M.J.
Perfettini J.	Ritchie P.A.	Simpson J.C.	Tinloi S.F.	Wilkey A.D.
Perks D.	Rittoo D.B.	Simpson M.E.	Tipping T.	Wilkinson P.A.
Perks J.S.	Roberts C.	Sinclair M.	Titoria M.	Will R.
Peterson A.C.	Roberts D.R.D.	Singh P.	Tofte B.C.	Williams A.C.
Peutrell J.M.	Roberts F.L.	Singh R.K.	Tolley M.E.	Williams C.
Phillips A.	Roberts P.	Skinner J.B.	Tomlinson J.H.	Williams D.J.M.
Phillips A.J.	Robertson S.M.	Smalberger J.M.	Tomlinson M.J.	Williams E.G.N.
Phillips D.C.	Robinson D.A.	Smith H.S.	Toomey P.	Williams L.J.
Phillips G.	Robinson K.N.	Smith I.D.	Trask M.D.	Williams P.J.
Phillips K.A.	Robson J.E.	Smith M.	Tring I.C.	Williams S.H.
Phillips P.D.	Rodgers R.C.	Smith M.B.	Trotter T.	Williams T.I.R.
Pick M.J.	Rogers C.	Smith P.A.	Turner D.A.B.	Wilson A.J.
Piggott S.E.	Rollin A.M.	Smyth P.R.F.	Turner R.J.N.	Wilson I.
Plumley M.H.	Rose N.	Sneyd J.R.	Turtle M.J.	Wilson P.T.J.
Plummer R.B.	Routh G.S.	Snow D.	Tweedie D.G.	Wiltshire S.J.
Pole Y.L.	Roylance J.	Somanathan S.	Ulyett I.	Windsor J.P.W.
Power K.J.	Royston D.	Somerville I.D.	Uncles D.R.	Woods S.D.
Pratt C.I.	Ruddock J.M.	Sowden G.R.	Underhill S.	Woodsford P.V.
Prince G.D.	Ruff S.J.	Spargo P.	Utting H.J.	Woollam C.H.M.
Protheroe D.T.	Ruiz K.	Spelina K.R.	Valentine J.	Wright M.M.
Pryle B.	Russell M.H.	Spencer E.M.	Valijan A.	Wyatt R.
Puddy B.R.	Russell W.	Spencer I.	van Miert M.	Yanny W.A.
Purcell G.	Ryall D.M.	Spiers S.P.W.	Van Ryssen M.E.P.	Yates D.W.
Purcell-Jones G.	Ryan D.A.	Spilsbury R.A.	Vanner R.G.	Yeoman P.
Putnam E.A.	Ryan T.D.R.	Sritharan S.	Vater M.	Young J.D.
Quaife J.	Saddler J.M.	Stacey M.R.	Venkat N.	Young P.N.
Radford P.	Sagar D.A.	Stacey R.G.W.	Ventham P.A.	Youssef H.
Raftery S.M.	Sahal B.B.	Stacey R.K.	Verghese C.	Zideman D.A.
Raghavjee I.V.	Saleh A.	Stannard C.	Verma R.	
Raithatha H.H.	Salmon N.P.	Stanton J.M.	Vine P.R.	
Raitt D.G.	Salt P.J.	Steer B.	Vohra A.	
Ralph S.	Samaan A.A.	Stevens J.	Voice A.	
Ralston S.	Samaan A.K.	Stock J.G.L.	Wadon C.A.	
Ramachandran A.	Sanchez A.	Stoneham J.R.	Wait C.M.	
Ramsden W.N.	Sanikop S.	Strang T.	Walker G.	
Rana M.S.	Sansome A.	Stray C.M.	Walker M.B.	
Ranasinghe D.	Saxena S.N.	Stride P.C.	Walker R.S.	
Randall N.P.C.	Scallan M.J.H.	Strong J.E.	Walker T.	
Randall P.J.	Schmulian C.M.	Strube P.	Wallbank W.A.	
Rao D.S.	Schofield N.M.	Stubbing J.F.	Walsh E.M.	
Rao I.N.	Schwarz P.A.	Sugden J.C.	Walters F.	
Raper J.M.	Scott A.D.	Summerfield R.J.	Walton D.P.	
Ravenscroft P.J.	Scott R.	Sutton B.A.	Walton M.	
Rawal S.B.	Scott-Knight V.	Swayne P.	Ward M.E.	
Ray S.	Seagger R.A.	Sweeney J.E.	Ward R.M.	
Razis P.A.	Searle A.E.	Swinhoe C.F.	Ward S.	

Appendix K - Participants

Consultant surgeons/gynaecologists

These consultant surgeons/gynaecologists returned at least one questionnaire relating to the period 1 April 1996 to March 1997.

Abel P.D.	Beacon J.P.	Browell D.	Cohen G.L.	Dhingra D.
Abrams P.	Bearn P.	Brown A.A.	Cole R.S.	Diamond T.
Ackroyd J.S.	Beeby D.I.	Brown G.J.A.	Colin J.F.	Dickerson D.
Adair H.M.	Beggs F.D.	Brown M.G.	Collins F.J.	Dixon A.R.
Adamson A.	Bell J.C.	Brown R.J.	Colmer M.R.	Docherty P.T.C.
Affifi R.	Bell M.S.	Brown S	Cook A.	Doig R.L.
Afify S.E.	Bell P.R.F.	Brown T.H.	Cook A.I.M.	Donaldson D.R.
Agarwal P.K.	Bellringer J.	Brunskill P.J.	Cooke R.S.	Donaldson R.A.
Agarwal P.N.	Benjamin J.C.	Buchanan G.	Cooksey G.	Donnelly R.J.
Agarwal S.	Benson E.A.	Budd D.W.G.	Cooper J.C.	Donovan R.
Aggarwal V.P.	Berry A.R.	Budd J.S.	Cooper M.J.	Dooley J.F.
Aitken R.H.	Best B.G.	Bull P.D.	Cooper Wilson M.	Dormandy J.A.
Alderman B.	Bett N.J.	Bulman C.H.	Corfield R.	Dornan J.C.
Aldoori M.I.	Betts C.D.	Bunker T.D.	Corrigan A.M.	Dossa M.
Alexander D.J.	Bevis C.R.A.	Burgess N.A.	Costello C.B.	Douglas D.L.
Ali D.	Bewick M.	Busfield H.M.B.	Cowen M.E.	Douglas P.S.
Ali M.L.	Billings P.J.	Butler C.	Cowie A.G.A.	Duke A.B.
Allan S.M.	Birch B.R.	Byrne P.O.	Cowie R.A.	Dunn D.C.
Allen M.	Birchall J.P.	Cade D.	Cox G.J.	Dunn M.
Allen N.	Birzgalis A.	Callaghan P.S.	Cox H.J.	Dunning J.
Alun-Jones T.	Bishop C.C.R.	Callum K.G.	Crabbe D.C.G.	Dunster G.D.
Amanat L.A.	Bishop M.C.	Calvert C.H.	Crane P.W.	Durham L.
Anderson G.E.	Bisson D.	Campbell J.B.	Cranley B.	Durning P.
Anderson I.D.	Black J.	Campbell W.B.	Cranston D.W.	Durrans D.
Anderson J.B.	Black J.E.	Carey D.	Crawshaw C.C.	Duthie J.
Anderson R.J.L.	Black P.D.	Carr R.T.W.	Crisp J.C.	Duthie J.S.
Andrews N.	Blackburn C.W.	Carroll R.N.P.	Cross A.T.	Dyke G.W.
Appleyard I.	Blacklock A.R.E.	Carswell W.	Crumplin M.K.H.	Dzumhur S.
Archbold J.A.	Blair S.D.	Carter P.G.	Cullen R.J.	Eardley I.
Archer T.J.	Blake J.R.S.	Case W.G.	Cumming J.A.	Earl P.D.
Armitage T.G.	Bloomfield M.D.	Cawthorn S.J.	Curley P.J.	Eaton A.C.
Armour R.H.	Bolger C.	Cetti N.E.	Curran F.T.	Ebbs S.R.
Ashworth M.F.	Bolger J.	Chan D.	Curry A.R.	Edge C.J.
Aukland P.	Bond E.B.	Chan K.K.	Curwen C.	Edmondson R.
Aylward G.W.	Booth C.M.	Chapman D.F.	Dahar N.A.	Edmondson S.
Badenoch D.F.	Borgaonkar S.S.	Chapman J.	Damale N.	Edwards J.L.
Bailey M.J.	Bose P.P.K.	Chappatte O.A.	Dan A.N.	Edwards M.H.
Bainbridge E.T.	Boughdady I.	Chapple C.R.	Das S.K.	Edwards P.
Baldwin D.L.	Boyd D.A.	Charnock F.M.L.	David V.C.	Eisenstein S.M.
Balfour T.W.	Boyd I.E.	Cheong-Leen P.	Davies M.	El-Shunnar K.S.
Ball A.	Boyd N.R.H.	Chia P.	Davies N.P.	Eldred J.M.
Ball A.J.	Boyd P.J.R.	Chilton C.P.	Dawson P.M.	Eldridge P.R.
Ball C.	Bradbrook R.A.	Chinegwundoh F.I.	Day J.B.	Elias J.
Bancewicz J.	Bradford R.	Chowdhury S.D.	De Bolla A.R.	Ellenbogen S.
Bannister J.J.	Bradley P.J.	Chumas P.D.	Deane A.M.	Ellis B.W.
Bardsley A.F.	Bradpiece H.A.	Clark J.	Deans G.	Emtage L.A.
Barr G.S.	Bramble F.J.	Clarke D.	de Boer F.	England P.C.
Barr H.	Brame K.G.	Clarke D.G.	Debrah S.	English P.J.
Barton D.	Bransom C.J.	Clarke S.	de Cossart L.M.	Enoch B.E.
Bashir E.	Brearley S.	Clarkson P.K.	Deiraniya A.	Evans A.S.
Bashir T.	Britton B.J.	Clayton J.K.	Denton G.W.L.	Evans B.T.
Bateman S.	Britton D.C.	Clearkin L.G.	Desai K.M.	Evans D.A.
Bates R.G.	Brooks J.	Clegg J.F.	Desmond A.D.	Evans G.H.
Batey N.R.	Brooks S.G.	Cobb R.A.	Devereux M.H.	Evans J.
Battersby R.D.E.	Brookstein R.	Cochrane J.P.S.	Dewar E.P.	Evans J.W.H.
Baxter J.N.	Brooman P.J.	Coen L.D.	Dhillon R.	Evans K.L.

Evans-Jones J.C.
Ewah P.O.
Eyong E.
Faber R.G.
Fairbank J.C.T.
Farrington W.T.
Fawcett I.
Feggetter J.G.W.
Fellows G.J.
Feneley R.C.L.
Fergus J.N.
Ferrie B.G.
Ferro M.
Field E.S.
Fielder C.
Fiennes A.
Fife D.G.
Finan P.J.
Flook D.
Fogarty P.
Forbes P.B.
Fordham M.
Fossard D.P.
Foster M.E.
Fountain S.
Fountain S.W.
Fowler C.G.
Fox G.C.
Fozard J.B.J.
Fraser I.A.
French M.E.
Frietes O.N.
Gajraj H.
Gallagher P.
Gallegos C.R.
Gammall M.M.
Gardner N.H.N.
Garlick D.J.
Garry R.
Gartell P.C.
Gatehouse D.
George P.P.
Ghanekar D.G.
Gibbens G.L.D.
Gibbons C.P.
Gillatt D.
Gilliland E.L.
Gillison E.W.
Gilroy D.
Gingell J.C.
Glazer G.
Glossop L.P.
Gogoi N.K.
Goldstraw P.
Goodall R.J.R.
Gooding M.R.
Goodman A.J.
Gordon A.
Gordon D.J.
Gordon E.M.
Gore R.
Gottlieb A.
Goulbourne I.A.
Gowland-Hopkins N.F.
Graham J.M.
Gray R.F.
Greatrex G.H.

Greenall M.
Greene D.
Greenway B.
Griffiths D.A.
Griffiths E.
Grimaldi P.M.G.
Grotte G.J.
Gudgeon M.
Guest J.
Gupta M.C.
Guy P.J.
Gwynn B.R.
Hackman B.W.
Hadley J.M.
Haggie S.J.
Hale J.E.
Hall J.H.
Hall R.I.
Halligan A.
Hallissey M.T.
Hamer D.B.
Hamid S.
Hammad Z.
Hammonds J.C.
Haque M.
Hardcastle J.D.
Hardingham M.
Harland R.N.L.
Harris D.L.
Harris V.G.
Harrison D.J.
Harrison G.S.M.
Harrison I.D.
Harrison J.D.
Harrison J.M.
Harrison S.C.W.
Harrison T.A.
Hart A.J.L.
Hart R.O.
Hartley M.
Harvey M.H.
Harvey-Hills N.
Hasan S.T.
Hastie K.J.
Hawkyard S.J.
Hay D.J.
Haynes S.
Hendry W.F.
Hendy-Ibbs P.M.
Hensher R.
Hershman M.
Heslip M.R.
Hibbert J.
Higgins A.F.
Higgins J.R.A.
Hill J.T.
Hindmarsh J.R.
Hobbiss J.H.
Hocken D.B.
Hodgkins J.
Hoile R.W.
Holbrook M.C.
Holcombe C.
Holden D.
Holdsworth P.J.
Holliday H.W.
Holme T.C.

Holmes F.J.
Holt S.D.H.
Hopkin N.B.
Hopkinson B.R.
Hopper M.S.C.
Horgan K.
Horner J.
Horrocks M.
Houghton D.J.
Houghton P.W.J.
Howard D.J.
Howat J.M.T.
Howell G.
Hudd C.
Huddy S.P.J.
Hughes-Nurse J.
Hulton N.R.
Hunter G.
Hurley P.
Hussain F.H.
Hussein I.Y.
Hutchinson C.
Hutchinson D.
Hutchinson I.F.
Iftikhar S.Y.
Ilankovan V.
Inglis J.A.
Ingoldby C.J.H.
Ingram G.
Ingram N.P.
Ireland D.
Ismal M.
Isworth R.A.
Jackson W.D.
Jacob G.
Jacobs I.
Jaganathan R.S.
Jago R.H.
Jain B.K.
Jakubowski J.
James M.J.
James S.E.
Jardine-Brown C.P.
Jasim S.
Jeffery P.J.
Jenkins B.
Jenkins D.H.R.
Jennison K.M.
Jepson K.
Jeyasingham K.
Johal B.
John D.G.
Johnson A.G.
Johnson A.O.B.
Johnson C.D.
Johnson D.A.N.
Johnson I.R.
Johnson J.R.
Johnson M.G.
Johnson S.R.
Johnston F.
Jones A.S.
Jones C.
Jones C.A.
Jones D.J.
Jones D.L.
Jones D.R.

Jones D.R.B.
Jones J.A.H.
Jones R.B.
Jones R.O.
Jones S.E.
Joseph T.
Joyce M.
Jurewicz A.
Kadow C.
Kane J.F.
Kapadia C.R.
Kapila L.
Karanjia N.
Karim O.
Kay N.J.
Keane P.
Kelleher J.P.
Kelly J.F.
Kelly S.B.
Kemeny A.A.
Kennedy C.L.
Kennedy R.H.
Kernohan R.
Kerr-Wilson R.
Khalil-Marzouk J.F.
Khan I.A.
Khan M.A.R.
Khan O.
Khazim R.M.
Kidd L.C.
Kinder R.B.
Kingston R.E.
Kirby R.S.
Kirkpatrick P.J.
Kitson J.
Kiwanuka A.I.
Klimach O.
Knight J.R.
Knight M.J.
Knox A.J.S.
Knox R.
Kobbe A.E.R.
Kolar K.M.
Kotta S.
Kourah M.A.
Kulkarni R.P.
Laing R.
Lake S.P.
Lamb R.J.
Lamerton A.J.
Lamki H.
Lane I.F.
Langdon J.D.
Langton J.
Larvin M.
Lavelle M.A.
Lawrence W.T.
Laws I.M.
Lawson R.A.M.
Lea R.E.
Leabeater B.F.
Lee J.O.
Lee M.D.
Lee P.W.R.
Lees T.A.
Leese T.
Le Fur R.

Lemberger R.J.
Lennox J.M.
Lennox M.S.
Leopard P.J.
Leopold P.W.
Leveckis J.
Lewis B.V.
Lewis J.L.
Lewis M.H.
Liston T.G.
Little G.
Liu S.
Livingstone J.
Lloyd D.A.
Lloyd D.M.
Longstaff S.
Loosemore T.
Lopes A.
Lotz J.C.
Loughridge W.G.G.
Love A.
Lowry J.C.
Lucas M.G.
Lund V.
Lyndon P.J.
Lyttle J.A.
McClelland R.
McCloy R.F.
McCollum C.N.
MacDermott S.
MacDonagh R.
MacDonald R.C.
McDonnell P.J.
MacFie J.
McGregor A.D.
McHugh D.
McIndoe A.
McIntosh I.H.
McKelvey S.T.D.
McKelvie P.
McKenna D.M.
MacKenzie I.
McKibbin A.
McLatchie G.
MacLennan I.
McLoughlin J.
McMahon M.J.
McMillan D.L.
McNeal A.D.
McNicholas T.A.
McRae A.R.
MacSweeney S.
McVicar I.
Mace M.C.
Machin D.G.
Mackle E.J.
Maclean A.D.W.
Macnab G.
Mahapatra T.K.
Maheson M.V.S.
Mair W.S.J.
Maiwand O.
Makin C.A.
Malak T.M.
Mansfield A.O.
Marcuson R.W.
Markham N.I.

Marsh H.T.
Marshall R.W.
Martin I.C.
Martin I.G.
Martin R.H.
Mason J.R.
Massey J.A.
Masson G.M.
Mathew B.G.
Maurice-Williams R.S.
Mavor A.I.D.
Maxwell R.J.
May A.R.L.
May R.E.
Maybury N.K.
Mearns A.J.
Mee A.D.
Meehan S.E.
Meer J.A.
Mehdian S.M.
Meleagros L.M.
Mellon J.K.
Menzies D.
Mercurius-Taylor L.A.
Meyrick Thomas J.
Michel M.
Milewski P.J.
Miller J.F.
Miller S.E.P.
Miller W.A.
Millner J.
Mills C.L.
Mills M.S.
Milner J.C.
Milton C.M.
Minchin A.J.
Mitchell D.C.
Modgill V.K.
Moghissi K.
Mohan J.
Moir A.A.
Moisey C.U.
Monaghan J.M.
Monson J.R.T.
Montgomery A.C.V.
Montgomery B.S.I.
Mooney P.
Moore A.J.
Moore K.T.H.
Moore P.J.
Moorehead R.J.
Moores W.K.
Moran B.
Morcos M.
Morgan M.W.E.
Morgan S.J.
Morgan W.E.
Morgan W.P.
Morrell M.T.
Morris G.E.
Morris I.R.
Morsman J.M.
Mortensen N.
Morton K.E.
Morton M.E.
Mosley J.G.
Mosquera D.A.

Mufti G.
Mughal M.M.
Mukoyogo J.M.
Mulholland R.C.
Mullan F.
Muller P.W.S.
Munson K.W.
Murphy D.J.
Murphy F.
Murrant N.J.
Murray A.
Murray A.
Murty G.
Musgrove B.
Narula A.
Nash A.G.
Nashef S.A.M.
Nasmyth D.G.
Naylor A.R.
Needham P.G.
Neil-Dwyer G.
Nelson I.W.
Nelson R.J.
Nicolaides A.
Noble A.D.
Noble J.G.
North A.D.
Norton R.
Nuseibeh I.
Nwabineli N.J.
O'Bonyo H.B.
O'Donoghue E.P.N.
O'Donoghue G.M.
O'Flynn K.
O'Hare M.F.
O'Reilly B.J.
O'Reilly P.H.
O'Riordan B.
O'Sullivan D.G.
Oram D.H.
Orr M.M.
Osborne D.R.
Osman I.S.
Ostick D.G.
Pace-Balzan A.
Padwick M.
Page R.D.
Pain J.A.
Palmer J.H.
Pantelides M.
Parker C.J.
Parker D.
Parr D.C.
Parr N.J.
Parrott N.R.
Parry J.R.W.
Parsons K.F.
Parvin S.
Parys B.T.
Pastorino U.
Paterson M.
Paterson M.E.L.
Patterson M.
Payne E.S.
Payne S.R.
Pearson H.J.
Pearson M.

Pearson R.C.
Peck J.E.
Peel K.R.
Peet T.N.D.
Pentlow B.D.
Pereira J.H.
Perkins C.
Perks A.G.B.
Perry S.
Peters J.
Phelan P.S.
Phillips J.G.
Phillips J.J.
Philp N.H.
Philp T.
Pickles J.M.
Pietroni M.C.
Pipe N.G.J.
Plail R.
Plumb A.P.
Pobereskin L.H.
Pocock R.D.
Pollard R.
Pope A.
Poskitt K.R.
Poston G.J.
Power R.
Prasad S.V.L.
Premachandra D.J.
Price J.H.
Primrose W.J.
Prince H.
Pritchett C.J.
Pushpanathan R.J.
Putnam G.D.
Pye J.K.
Pyper P.C.
Queen K.B.
Rahamim J.
Rainsbury R.M.
Rajasekaran J.
Rajesh P.B.
Ralphs D.N.L.
Ramsden C.
Ramus N.I.
Randall C.J.
Rangecroft R.G.
Ranjit R.
Rao P.N.
Rashid A.
Ratliff D.A.
Ravi M.
Ravichandran G.
Reddy P.
Reed M.W.
Rees A.
Rees A.E.
Rees M.
Regan P.
Reid B.A.
Reid D.
Reilly D.
Reilly P.G.
Resouly A.
Reynolds R.
Rhind R.
Rhodes M.

Rhys-Williams S.
Richards P.
Richardson J.A.
Richmond W.D.
Ridley D.
Rigby C.C.
Rigg K.M.
Ritchie A.
Ritchie A.W.S.
Roberts A.
Roberts J.G.
Robertshaw J.K.
Robertson A.A.
Robertson C.
Robinson A.C.
Robinson M.H.
Robinson M.R.G.
Roe A.M.
Rogawski K.M.
Rogers J.
Rooney P.S.
Rose M.B.
Rosen E.
Rosenberg D.A.
Rosin M.D.
Rosin R.D.
Ross A.C.
Ross A.H.M.
Ross S.A.
Rothera M.P.
Rothwell N.
Rowlands D.J.
Rowse A.D.
Rowson N.J.
Royston C.M.S.
Rundle J.S.H.
Sabanathan S.
Sabharwal S.
Sabin H.I.
Sadler A.P.
Sagar P.M.
Sagar S.
Sainsbury J.R.C.
Salter M.C.P.
Sampath S.A.C.
Samuel P.R.
Sandeman D.R.
Sanderson C.J.
Sandhu D.P.S.
Sansom J.R.
Sant Cassia L.J.
Sarkar P.K.
Sarmah B.D.
Saunders N.R.
Sauven P.
Savage P.E.
Sayer R.E.
Sayer T.
Scott A.D.N.
Scott G.I.
Scott I.H.K.
Scott I.V.
Scott N.
Scott R.A.P.
Scott S.D.
Scriven M.
Sell P.J.

Sells R.A.
Sellu D.
Sengupta B.S.
Sergeant R.J.
Shafi M.I.
Shafiq M.
Shaikh N.A.
Shan S.
Shanahan D.J.
Sharma N.
Sharma P.
Sharma S.D.
Sharma S.K.
Sharp J.
Shaw G.
Shepherd R.J.
Sherlock D.J.
Sherman I.W.
Shieff C.L.
Shields M.D.
Shinkfield M.
Shortridge R.T.J.
Sibson D.E.
Sill P.R.
Silverman S.H.
Silvester K.C.
Simms J.M.
Singh A.
Singh A.B.
Singh G.
Sinha K.N.
Smallpeice C.J.
Smith E.M.
Smith M.R.
Smith R.B.
Smyth A.G.
Snow D.G.
Sole G.M.
Soorae A.S.
Sosnowski A.W.
South L.M.
Sowinski A.
Speakman C.T.
Spearing G.J.
Spencer S.R.
Spencer T.S.
Spychal R.T.
Spyt T.
Srinivasan V.
Staff W.G.
Stafford F.W.
Stafford N.D.
Stansby G.
Stassen L.F.A.
Stebbing M.A.
Steel M.R.
Steele R.J.C.
Steele S.C.
Stewart D.J.
Stewart J.
Stewart P.A.H.
Stewart W.E.
Stoddard C.J.
Stoker T.A.M.
Stoodley B.J.
Stower M.J.
Strachan J.R.

Strachan R.D.
Stringer R.
Stuart A.E.
Studley J.
Sturzaker H.G.
Sudlow R.A.
Sullivan S.C.
Suresh G.
Surtees P.
Sutton R.
Swingler G.
Symes J.M.
Taggart D.
Tait W.F.
Talbot R.W.
Tate J.J.T.
Taylor A.B.W.
Taylor M.C.
Taylor P.H.
Taylor S.A.
Taylor W.G.
Teddy P.J.
Terry T.R.
Thomas D.M.
Thomas D.R.
Thomas M.H.
Thomas W.E.G.
Thompson H.H.
Thompson J.F.
Thompson M.H.
Thomson A.A.G.
Thomson H.J.
Thorpe A.C.
Thorpe J.A.C.
Thurston A.V.
Timoney A.
Tindall S.F.
Tolley N.
Toor K.S.
Tophill P.R.
Towler J.M.
Townsend E.R.
Toynton C.J.
Treacy P.J.
Treble N.J.
Trotter G.
Tulloch D.N.
Turner A.G.
Turner D.T.L.
Turner S.M.
Tweedie J.H.
Tyrrell M.R.
Upadhyay S.
Upsdell S.M.
Urwin G.H.
Vadanan B.S.
Van Vuuren L.
Vandal M.T.
Vanwaeyenbergh J.
Vasey D.P.
Vaughan E.D.
Vaughan R.
Veitch P.S.
Vesey S.G.
Vetrivel S.M.
Vipond M.
Virdi J.

Wake M.
Walker M.G.
Walker R.T.
Walker S.J.
Wallace D.M.A.
Wallace R.G.H.
Wallwork J.
Walsh S.
Walsh T.H.
Ward D.
Ward D.C.
Ward J.K.
Ward S.E.
Watkin D.F.L.
Watkins R.M.
Watson C.
Watson D.C.T.
Watson G.M.
Watson J.A.S.
Watson M.G.
Way B.G.
Waymont B.
Webb J.K.
Webb P.J.
Webber P.A.
Wedgwood K.R.
Weeden D.
Wells A.D.
Wells F.C.
Wellwood J.M.
Wengraf C.L.
Westmore G.A.
Weston P.M.T.
Weston Underwood J.
Westwood C.A.
White B.D.
White C.M.
Whitehead E.
Whitehead S.M.
Whiteley G.S.W.
Whiteway J.E.
Whitfield B.C.S.
Whyman M.R.
Wickham M.H.
Wilkins D.C.
Wilkinson M.J.S.
Willatt D.J.
Williams G T
Williams G.
Williams G.T.
Williams H.
Williams H.T.
Williams J.H.
Williams J.L.
Williams M.R.
Williams T.G.
Williamson B.
Williamson E.P.M.
Wills M.I.
Wilson L.
Wilson N.M.
Wilson R.Y.
Wilson-McDonald J.
Windle R.
Winslet M.C.
Witherow R.O.N.
Womack N.

Woods W.
Woodward A.
Woodwards R.T.
Woolfenden K.A.
Worth P.H.L.
Worth R.W.
Wyatt M.G.
Wynne K.S.
Yacoub M.H.
Yardley M.P.J.
Yeo R.
Young H.L.
Young K.
Zaidi A.A.
Zygmunt S.C.

Appendix L – Local Reporters

This list shows the local reporters as of August 1998.

We recognise that there are many clinical audit and information departments involved in providing data, although we have in many cases named only the consultant clinician nominated as local reporter.

Anglia & Oxford

Addenbrooke's	Dr D. Wight
Bedford Hospital	Mrs S. Blackley
Heatherwood & Wexham Park Hospitals	Dr M.H. Ali
Hinchingbrooke Health Care	Dr M.D. Harris
Ipswich Hospital	Mr I.E. Cowles
James Paget Hospital	Mrs C.L. Eagle
Kettering General Hospital	Dr B.E. Gostelow
Kings Lynn & Wisbech Hospitals	Miss J.M. Rippon
Milton Keynes General	Dr S.S. Jalloh
Norfolk & Norwich Health Care	Dr A.J.G. Gray
Northampton General Hospital	Dr A.J. Molyneux
Nuffield Orthopaedic Centre	Dr P. Millard
Oxford Radcliffe Hospital	Dr P. Millard (John Radcliffe Hospital)
	Dr M.J. Mahy (Horton General Hospital)
Papworth Hospital	Dr N. Cary
Peterborough Hospitals	Dr P.M. Dennis
Radcliffe Infirmary	Dr P. Millard
Royal Berkshire & Battle Hospital	Dr R. Menai-Williams
South Buckinghamshire	Dr M.J. Turner
Stoke Mandeville Hospital	Dr A.F. Padel
The Luton & Dunstable Hospital	Dr D.A.S. Lawrence
West Suffolk Hospitals	Mrs V. Hamilton

North Thames

Basildon & Thurrock General Hospitals	Dr S.G. Subbuswamy
Central Middlesex Hospital	Dr C.A. Amerasinghe
Chase Farm Hospitals	Dr W.H.S. Mohamid
Chelsea & Westminster Healthcare	Ms G. Nuttal
Ealing Hospital	Dr C. Schmulian
East Hertfordshire	Dr A. Fattah
Essex Rivers Healthcare	Mrs A. Bridge
Forest Healthcare	Dr K.M. Thomas

Hammersmith Hospitals	Professor G.W.H. Stamp (No local reporter for Charing Cross Hospital)
Havering Hospitals	Ms C. Colley
Hillingdon Hospital	Dr F.G. Barker
Mid-Essex Hospital Services	Mr A.H.M. Ross (Broomfield Hospital) Dr S.G. Subbuswamy (St Andrew's Hospital)
Moorfields Eye Hospital	Professor P. Luthert
Mount Vernon & Watford Hospitals	Mrs M. Hill (Mount Vernon Hospital) Dr W.K. Blenkinsopp (Watford General Hospital)
Newham Healthcare	Dr G. Russell
North Hertfordshire	Dr D.J. Madders
North Middlesex Hospital	Dr K.J. Jarvis
Northwick Park & St Mark's	Dr S. Boyle
Redbridge Healthcare	Dr P. Tanner
Royal Brompton & Harefield Hospitals	Ms J. Byrne (Harefield Hospital) Professor R. Denison (Royal Brompton Hospital)
Royal Free Hampstead	Dr J.E. McLaughlin
Royal Marsden Hospital	Mr R.J. Shearer
Royal National Orthopaedic Hospital	None
Southend Health Care	Ms L. Bell
St Albans & Hemel Hempstead	Dr A.P. O'Reilly
St Mary's Hospital	Ms R.A. Hittinger
The Great Ormond Street Hospital for Children	Dr A. Mackersie
The Homerton Hospital	Ms M. Joseet
The Princess Alexandra Hospital	Dr R.G.M. Letcher
The Royal Hospitals	Dr P.J. Flynn
University College London Hospitals	Ms A.E. Glover (Middlesex Hospital Mrs J.A. Sullivan (The National Hospital for Neurology and Neurosurgery)
Wellhouse	Dr J. El-Jabbour
West Middlesex University Hospital	Dr R.G. Hughes
Whittington Hospital	Dr S. Ramachandra

North West

Aintree Hospitals	Dr W. Taylor
Blackburn, Hyndburn & Ribble Valley Healthcare	Mr R.W. Nicholson
Blackpool Victoria Hospital	Dr K.S. Vasudev
Bolton Hospitals	Dr S. Wells
Burnley Health Care	Mr D.G.D. Sandilands
Bury Health Care	Dr E. Herd
Central Manchester Healthcare	Dr E.W. Benbow
Chorley & South Ribble	Dr C. Loyden

North West continued

Christie Hospital	None
Countess of Chester Hospital	Dr P.R.M. Steele
East Cheshire	Dr A.R. Williams
Halton General Hospital	Dr K. Strahan
Liverpool Women's Hospital	Ms C. Fox
Manchester Children's Hospitals	Dr M. Newbould
Mid Cheshire Hospitals	Miss H. Moulton
Morecambe Bay Hospitals	Dr R.W. Blewitt (Royal Lancaster Infirmary)
	Dr V.M. Joglekar (Furness General Hospital)
North Manchester Health Care	None
Oldham	Dr I. Seddon
Preston Acute Hospitals	Dr C.M. Nicholson
Rochdale Healthcare	Mr S. Murray
Royal Liverpool & Broadgreen University Hospital	Miss K. Scott
Royal Liverpool Children's Hospital	Mrs P.A. McCormack
Salford Royal Hospitals	Mr M. McKenna
South Manchester University Hospitals	Dr J. Coyne (Withington Hospital)
	Dr P.S. Hasleton (Wythenshawe Hospital)
Southport & Formby	Dr S.A.C. Dundas
St Helens & Knowsley Hospitals	Mr K. Benyon
Stockport Acute Services	Dr P. Meadows
Tameside Acute Care	Dr A.J. Yates
The Cardiothoracic Centre Liverpool	Mr M. Jackson
Trafford Healthcare	Dr B.N.A. Hamid
Walton Centre for Neurology & Neurosurgery	Dr J. Broome
Warrington Hospital	Dr M.S. Al-Jafari
West Lancashire	Mr A.D. Johnson
Wigan & Leigh Health Services	Ms S. Tarbuck
Wirral Hospital	Dr M.B. Gillett
Wrightington Hospital	Mr A.D. Johnson

Northern & Yorkshire

Airedale	Dr J.J. O'Dowd
Bradford Hospitals	Dr B. Naylor
Calderdale Healthcare	Mr R.J.R. Goodall
Carlisle Hospitals	Dr E.D. Long
City Hospitals Sunderland	Miss K. Ramsey
Dewsbury Health Care	Dr P. Gudgeon
East Yorkshire Community Healthcare	Mr G. Britchford
East Yorkshire Hospitals	Mr G. Britchford
Gateshead Hospitals	Dr I.M.J. Mathias

Harrogate Health Care	Miss A.H. Lawson
Hartlepool & East Durham	Mrs A. Lister
Huddersfield	Dr H.H. Ali
Newcastle upon Tyne Hospitals	Dr M.K. Bennett
	Miss D. Robson
North Durham Healthcare	Dr D. Wood
North Tees Health	Dr J. Hoffman
Northallerton Health Services	Dr D.C. Henderson
Northumbria Healthcare	Dr J.A. Henry (Cheviot & Wansbeck)
	Dr F. Johri (North Tyneside)
Pinderfields & Pontefract Hospitals	Dr S. Gill (Pinderfields General Hospital)
	Dr I.W.C. MacDonald (Pontefract General Infirmary)
Royal Hull Hospitals	Dr M.R.F. Reynolds
Scarborough & N E Yorkshire Healthcare	Dr A.M. Jackson
South Durham Healthcare	Dr D.C.A. Senadhira (Bishop Auckland Hospital)
	Ms C. Evans (Darlington Memorial)
South Tees Acute Hospitals	Mrs L. Black
South Tyneside Healthcare	Dr K.P. Pollard
United Leeds Teaching Hospitals	Dr C. Abbott (The General Infirmary at Leeds)
	Mr S. Knight (St James' University Hospital)
West Cumbria Health Care	Dr R.G. Ghazala
York Health Services	Dr C. Bates

South Thames

Ashford & St Peter's Hospitals	Dr J.C. Dawson (Ashford Hospital)
	Mr R.H. Moore (St Peter's Hospital)
Brighton Healthcare	Mr M. Renshaw
Bromley Hospitals	Dr M.H. Elmahallawy
Dartford & Gravesham	Dr A.T.M. Rashid
Eastbourne Hospitals	Mr M.D. Bastable
Epsom Health Care	Dr T.J. Matthews
Frimley Park Hospital	Dr G.F. Goddard
Greenwich Healthcare	Mr O. Smith
Guy's & St Thomas'	Dr. B. Hartley (Guy's Hospital)
	Professor S.B. Lucas (St Thomas' Hospital)
Hastings & Rother	Mr S. Ball
Kent & Canterbury Hospitals	Mr M. Guarino
Kent & Sussex Weald	Dr G.A. Russell
King's Healthcare	Mr M. Fleming
Kingston Hospital	Mr P. Willson
Mayday Health Care	Mr C. Fernandez
Medway	Mrs J.L. Smith

South Thames continued

Mid Kent Healthcare	Mr J. Vickers
Mid-Sussex	Dr P.A. Berresford (The Princess Royal Hospital) Mr P.H. Walter (Hurstwood Park Neurology Centre)
Queen Mary's Sidcup	Dr E.J.A. Aps
Richmond, Twickenham & Roehampton	Mr M. McSweeney
Royal Surrey County & St Luke's Hospitals	Mrs M. Davies
South Kent Hospitals	Dr C.W. Lawson
St George's Healthcare	Dr S. Dilly
Surrey & Sussex Healthcare	Ms C. Parkinson (East Surrey Hospital) Dr C. Moon (Crawley Hospital and Horsham Hospital)
Thanet Healthcare	Mrs B.M. Smith
The Lewisham Hospital	Dr C. Keen
The Queen Victoria Hospital	Mrs D.M. Helme
The Royal West Sussex	Mr J.N.L. Simson
The St Helier	Dr E.H. Rang
Worthing & Southlands Hospitals	Mrs J. Tofield

South & West

Dorset Community	Dr A. Anscombe
East Gloucestershire	Dr W.J. Brampton
East Somerset	Dr G. Purcell
Frenchay Healthcare	Dr N.B.N. Ibrahim
Gloucestershire Royal	Dr B.W. Codling
Isle of Wight Healthcare	Mr P. Donaldson
North Hampshire Hospitals	Dr J.M. Finch
Northern Devon Healthcare	Dr J. Davies
Plymouth Hospitals	Dr C.B.A. Lyons
Poole Hospital	Dr D.S. Nicholas
Portsmouth Hospitals	Dr N.J.E. Marley
Royal Bournemouth & Christchurch Hospitals	Mr E. Robbin
Royal Cornwall Hospitals	Dr R. Pitcher
Royal Devon & Exeter Healthcare	Dr R.H.W. Simpson
Royal United Hospital Bath	None
Salisbury Health Care	Dr C.E. Fuller
South Devon Healthcare	Dr D.W. Day
Southampton University Hospitals	Dr A. Bateman
Southmead Health Services	Ms G. Davies
Swindon & Marlborough Hospital	Mr M.H. Galea
Taunton & Somerset	Mr I. Eyre-Brook
United Bristol Healthcare	Dr E.A. Sheffield
West Dorset General Hospitals	Dr A. Anscombe

| Weston Area Health | Dr M.F. Lott |
| Winchester & Eastleigh Healthcare | Dr R.K. Al-Talib |

Trent

Barnsley District General Hospital	Dr M.A. Longan
Bassetlaw Hospital & Community Services	Dr P.A. Parsons
Central Nottinghamshire Health Care	Dr. I. Ross
Central Sheffield University Hospitals	Dr C Angel
Chesterfield & North Derbyshire Royal Hospital	Dr P.B. Gray
Southern Derbyshire Hospitals	Mrs L. Smith (Deby City General Hospital)
	Mr J.R. Nash (Derbyshire Royal Infirmary)
Doncaster Royal Infirmary & Montagu Hospital	Dr J.A.H. Finbow
Glenfield Hospital	Mrs S. Clarke
Grantham & District Hospital	Dr D. Clark
Leicester General Hospital	Dr E.H. Mackay
Leicester Royal Infirmary	Mr R. Mowbray
Lincoln & Louth	Dr J.A. Harvey (Lincoln County Hospital)
	Mr E.O. Amaku (County Hospital Louth)
North East Lincolnshire	Dr W.M. Peters
Northern General Hospital	Dr S.K. Suvarna
Nottingham City Hospital	Dr. J.R. Jones
Pilgrim Health	Ms S. Cosgriff
Queen's Medical Centre University Hospital	Dr. J.R. Jones
Rotherham General Hospitals	Mr R.B. Jones
Scunthorpe & Goole Hospitals	Dr C.M. Hunt
Sheffield Children's Hospital	Dr I. Barker
The King's Mill Centre for Health Care Services	Ms J. Jenkins
West Lindsey	Dr J.A. Harvey

West Midlands

Alexandra Healthcare	Dr L. Brown
Birmingham Children's Hospital	Dr F. Raafat
Birmingham Heartlands Hospital	Dr M. Taylor
Birmingham Women's Healthcare	Dr T. Rollason
Burton Hospitals	Dr N. Kasthuri
George Eliot Hospital	Dr J. Mercer
Good Hope Hospital	Dr J. Hull
Hereford Hospitals	Dr F. McGinty
Kidderminster Health Care	Dr G.H. Eeles
Mid Staffordshire General Hospitals	Dr V. Suarez

West Midlands continued

North Staffordshire Hospital Centre	Dr T.A. French
Robert Jones & Agnes Hunt	Mrs C. McPherson
Royal Shrewsbury Hospitals	Dr R.A. Fraser
Sandwell Healthcare	Dr J. Simon
South Warwickshire General Hospitals	Mr M. Gilbert
The City Hospital	None
The Dudley Group of Hospitals	Dr S. Ghosh
The Princess Royal Hospital	Dr R.A. Fraser
The Royal Orthopaedic Hospital	Mr A. Thomas
The Royal Wolverhampton Hospitals	Dr J. Tomlinson
University Hospital Birmingham	Professor E.L. Jones (Queen Elizabeth Hospital) (No local reporter for Selly Oak Hospital)
Walsall Hospitals	Dr Y.L. Hock
Walsgrave Hospitals	Dr J. Macartney
Worcester Royal Infirmary	Mr A. Singfield

Northern Ireland

Altnagelvin Hospitals	Dr J.N. Hamilton
Armagh & Dungannon	Mr B. Cranley
Belfast City Hospital	Mr R. J. Hannon
Causeway	Dr C. Watters
Craigavon Area Hospital Group	Mr B. Cranley
Down Lisburn	Dr B. Huss (Lagan Valley Hospital) Mrs M. Gilgunn (Downe Hospital)
Green Park Healthcare	Dr J. D. Connolly
Mater Hospital	Dr P. Gormley
Newry & Mourne	Mr B. Cranley
Sperrin Lakeland	Dr W. Holmes (Erne Hospital) Dr F. Robinson (Tyrone County Hospital)
The Royal Group of Hospitals & Dental Hospitals	Ms M. Toner
Ulster Community & Hospital	Dr T. Boyd
United Hospitals	Mr I. Garstin (Antrim Area Hospital) Mr P.C. Pyper (Mid -Ulster Hospital) Mr D. Gilroy (Whiteabbey Hospital)

Wales

Bridgend & District	Dr A.M. Rees
Carmarthen & District	Dr R.B. Denholm
Ceredigion & Mid Wales	Mrs C. Smith
East Glamorgan	Dr D. Stock
Glan Clwyd District General Hospital	Dr B. Rogers
Glan Hafren	None

Glan-y-Mor	Dr A. Dawson
Gwynedd Hospitals	Dr M. Hughes
Llandough Hospital & Community	Dr J. Gough
Llanelli Dinefwr	Dr L.A. Murray
Morriston Hospital/Ysbyty Treforys	Dr A. Dawson
Nevill Hall & District	Dr R.J. Kellett
North Glamorgan	None
Pembrokeshire & Derwen	Dr G.R. Melville Jones
Rhondda Health Care	Dr D. Stock
Swansea	Dr S. Williams
University Hospital of Wales	Dr A.G. Douglas-Jones (University Hospital of Wales)
	Mrs P. Perrott (Cardiff Royal Infirmary)
Wrexham Maelor Hospital	Dr R.B. Williams

Defence Medical Services

The Duchess of Kent Military Hospital	The Commanding Officer
The Royal Naval Hospital, Haslar	Dr N. Carr

Guernsey / Isle of Man / Jersey

Guernsey	Dr B.P. Gunton-Bunn
Isle of Man	Ms E. Clark
Jersey	Dr H. Goulding

BUPA

BUPA Wellesley Hospital	Mrs L. Horner
BUPA Hospital Norwich	Ms J. Middows
BUPA Hospital Leeds	Mr D. Farrell
BUPA Hospital Little Aston	Mr K. Smith
BUPA North Cheshire Hospital	Miss A.L. Alexander
BUPA Parkway Hospital	Mrs M.T. Hall
BUPA Hospital Portsmouth	Ms J. Ward
BUPA Roding Hospital	Ms D. Brett
BUPA Hospital Hull & East Riding	Ms A. Meyer
BUPA South Bank Hospital	Mrs F. Cox
BUPA Hospital Leicester	Mrs C.A. Jones
BUPA Hospital Elland	Ms M.E. Schofield
BUPA St. Saviour's Hospital	Mrs E. Biddle
BUPA Belvedere Hospital	Mr S.J. Greatorex
BUPA Hospital Manchester	Ms A. McArdle
BUPA Hartswood Hospital	Ms N. Howes
The Glen Hospital	Miss M. O'Toole

BUPA continued

BUPA Alexandra Hospital	Mr N.R. Permain
BUPA Hospital Bushey	Ms L. Adair
BUPA Cambridge Lea Hospital	Ms M. Vognsen
BUPA Gatwick Park Hospital	Mrs D. Wright
BUPA Murrayfield Hospital	Mr S. Milner
BUPA Hospital Harpenden	Ms B. Hayter
BUPA Hospital Cardiff	Dr A. Gibbs
BUPA Fylde Coast Hospital	Ms D. Revell
BUPA Dunedin Hospital	Mrs C. Bude
BUPA Hospital Clare Park	Ms M. Wood
BUPA Chalybeate Hospital	Ms M. Falconer

General Healthcare Group

The Priory Hospital	Dr A.G. Jacobs
AMI Princess Margaret Hospital	Mrs J. Bevington
Harbour Hospital	Ms S. Prince
The Runnymede Hospital	Mrs P. Hill
The Somerfield Hospital	Ms N. Poulson
Chelsfield Park Hospital	Ms C. Poll
The Wellington Hospital	Mr R.J. Hoff
Fawkham Manor Hospital	Mrs C. Pagram
The Sloane Hospital	Mrs U. Palmer
Clementine Churchill Hospital	Dr I. Chanarin
The Thornbury Hospital	Mrs J. Cooper
The Princess Grace Hospital	Ms D. Cunliffe
The Chiltern Hospital	Ms S. Hill
The Harley Street Clinic	Ms S. Thomas
The Highfield Hospital	Mr C.J. Durkin
Park Hospital	Ms S. Quickmire
The Blackheath Hospital	Ms V. Power
The Portland Hospital for Women and	Miss A.D. Sayburn
Alexandra Hospital	Mrs P. Enstone
The Chaucer Hospital	Mrs G. Mann

Nuffield

The North London Nuffield Hospital	Miss J. Ward
The Huddersfield Nuffield Hospital	Miss S. Panther
The Grosvenor Nuffield Hospital	Mrs J.L. Whitmore
The Lancaster & Lakeland Nuffield Hospital	Miss A. Durbin
The Nuffield Hospital Leicester	Mrs S. Harriman

Mid Yorkshire Nuffield Hospital	Mrs M. Dunderdale
The Newcastle Nuffield Hospital	Miss K.C. Macfarlane
The Hull Nuffield Hospital	Ms V. Ward
The North Staffordshire Nuffield Hospital	Mr D. Allison
The Nuffield Hospital Plymouth	Mrs T. Starling
The Purey Cust Nuffield Hospital	Mr J. Gdaniec
The Shropshire Nuffield Hospital	Mrs S. Crossland
The Somerset Nuffield Hospital	Mrs J.A. Dyer
The Sussex Nuffield Hospital	Mrs F. Booty
The Woking Nuffield Hospital	Miss B.E. Harrison
The Thames Valley Nuffield Hospital	Ms D. Williams
The Acland Hospital	Miss C. Gilbert
The Exeter Nuffield Hospital	Mrs A. Turnbull
The Tunbridge Wells Nuffield Hospital	Mr R. Muddiman
The Wolverhampton Nuffield Hospital	Mrs I. Jones
The Wessex Nuffield Hospital	Mrs V. Heckford
The Wye Valley Nuffield Hospital	Mrs W.P. Mawdesley
HRH Princess Christian's Hospital	Ms S. Fisher
The Birmingham Nuffield Hospital	Mrs P. Shields
The Bournemouth Nuffield Hospital	Mrs S. Jackson
The Chesterfield Nuffield Hospital	Miss P.J. Bunker
The East Midlands Nuffield Hospital	Mrs C. Williams
The Cotswold Nuffield Hospital	Mrs J.T. Penn
The Duchy Nuffield Hospital	Miss S.J. Gardner
The Cleveland Nuffield Hospital	Mrs S. Jelley
The Essex Nuffield Hospital	Mrs B.M. Parker
The Warwickshire Nuffield Hospital	Mrs J. Worth
London Bridge Hospital	Ms Y. Terry

St Martin's Hospitals

The Lister Hospital	Mrs J. Johnson
Devonshire Hospital	Miss C. Lewington

Other independent hospitals

Benenden Hospital	Mr D. Hibler
The London Clinic	Mrs K. Perkins